PRAYERS OF OUR HEARTS
in word and action

This book is dedicated to
Abigail and Jonathan
who died in infancy,
John and Michael
who will not be forgotten,
and to all who struggle to pray.

~ ‡ ~

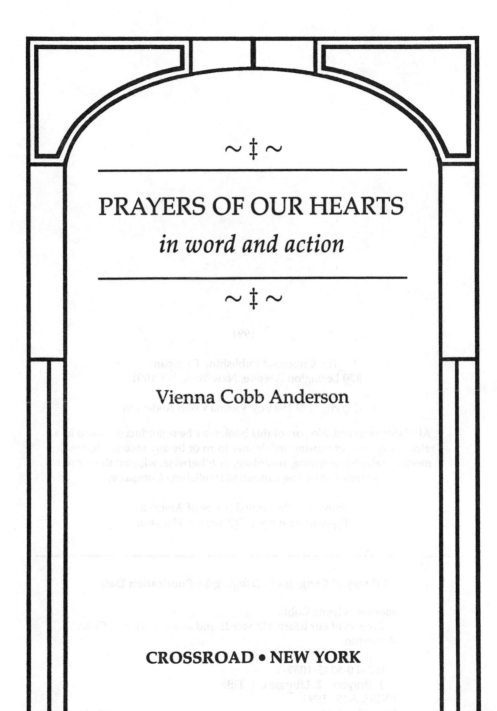

~ ‡ ~

PRAYERS OF OUR HEARTS
in word and action

~ ‡ ~

Vienna Cobb Anderson

CROSSROAD • NEW YORK

1991

The Crossroad Publishing Company
370 Lexington Avenue, New York, NY 10017

Copyright © 1991 by Vienna Cobb Anderson

Printed in the United States of America
Typesetting output: TEXSource, Houston

Library of Congress Cataloging-in-Publication Data

Anderson, Vienna Cobb.
    Prayers of our hearts : in words and action / Vienna Cobb
Anderson.
        p. cm.
    ISBN 0-8245-1059-3
    1. Prayers. 2. Liturgies. I. Title.
BV245.A45 1991
264'.13—dc20   90-22541
                                                        CIP

Contents

PRAYERS FOR THE HUMAN FAMILY

PRAYERS FOR THOSE WHO ARE SICK

PRAYERS FOR THE DEPARTED

OTHER PRAYERS

LITTLE CHILDREN'S PRAYERS

CHILDREN'S RITUALS

Introduction

Many have grown weary, as I have, of waiting a lifetime for the Church to include the longings of our hearts in words that are inclusive and in liturgies that reflect the changes of our lives. Week after week, many of us have been burdened by the weight of a language that neither names our dreams, struggles, or sorrows, nor offers us the consolation of feeling named or affirmed as full members of the Body of Christ.

Some individuals have left the community of the Church; they think they have lost their faith since the language of worship seems so foreign to the longings, doubts, and fears of their hearts. Others wouldn't dream of entering through the door, assuming that whatever happens inside is archaic and irrelevant to their own life experiences.

Indeed, to me the tragedy of liturgy today is that we have made the language of worship so abstract that it is nearly impossible to sense the joy and blessing of life in an earthy and real way. We neither laugh nor weep in Church, and that is a great pity that robs us of a deeper compassion for others and diminishes our own living.

The most recent edition of the *Book of Common Prayer* of the Episcopal Church, like many new books of worship, does not contain prayers that relate to issues that affect us all: child abuse, violent crime, rape, terrorism, divorce, and AIDS, to name but a few of today's concerns for humankind. During the period of sweeping liturgical change in all denominations during the 1960s and 1970s, words were shuffled on paper by scholars, but the cries of seekers for a new language of prayer went largely unheard.

It is to help in the process of filling this gap in our liturgical life that I have written this book of rituals and prayers. It is not intended to take the place of any denomination's book of worship, but to be a supplement to them. I have never considered myself a writer; indeed, I am often embarrassed when I express myself so personally in a public way. The writing of these prayers has been a spiritual journey for me beyond the barriers of my own fears and inadequacies; for this journey in faith I give thanks to God and to all the women, men, and children whose joys and sorrows have touched my heart and whose lives have contributed to the writing of these prayers and liturgies. I give special thanks to Sally Bucklee for her encouragement to create the genesis of this work of inclusive prayers for the Episcopal Women's Caucus at the Lambeth Conference in Canterbury, England, in the summer of 1988; Fred Hartley, who died during the course of the writing and who inspired many prayers; Judy Bowes, who journeyed with me during the struggle to name God using feminine images; the Rev. Dr. William A. Wendt, my mentor and friend who taught me it was all right to risk, to fail, and to celebrate all the while; the Rt. Rev. John T. Walker, the former Bishop of the Diocese of Washington, who gave me permission to explore new possibilities for corporate worship; the Rt. Rev. Desmond Tutu, who has been a sign of hope in this troubled world; Abigail Dokken-Tourish, whose brief life began and ended too soon and who taught me so much about life's meanings and blessings in the five tumultuous months she lived; Michael Pleasants whose courage in the face of death has been a blessing to me and to all the people of St. Margaret's; and the Platt family, whose wonderful "Little House" in North Haven, Maine, was the perfect retreat for writing this book.

I owe a deep sense of gratitude to the members of the Community of Hagar who supported me in the journey to become more inclusive in word and action that preceded this work. They are the source and inspiration for the Canon of the Eucharist that is included in this book. I thank the people of St. Margaret's for their love and support and for the vacations that gave me the time to complete this collection of prayers, liturgies, and rituals.

To Robert Heller, Frank Oveis, and all the editors at Crossroad/ Continuum whose help, assistance, and encouragement have been invaluable, I am deeply grateful.

I encourage you, the reader, to use these offerings in the way that best suits your needs and to alter the words as necessary to help you to pray. I seek your forgiveness for my failure to express the prayers of your heart, which may be omitted here. I hope you will join me in writing prayers that will enable the Church to continue the process of including all in lifting our hearts to God.

May your lives be enriched and blessed as God's Spirit leads you in prayer, as I have been blessed through this endeavor of creation.

North Haven, Maine
July 1990

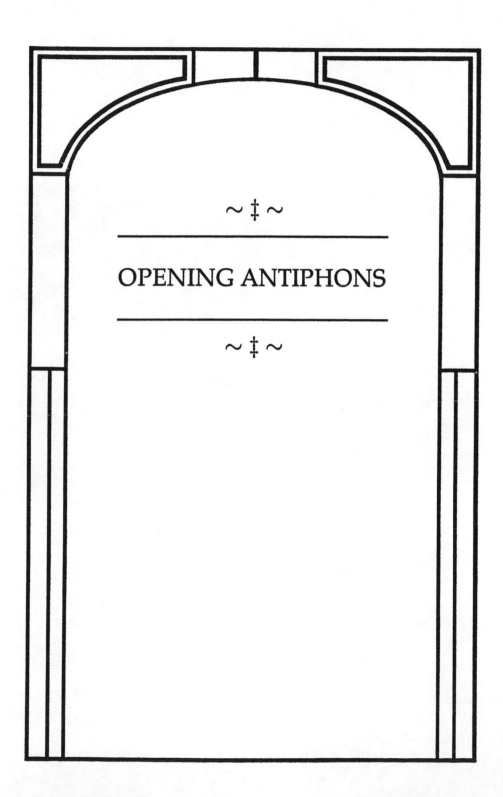

~ ‡ ~

OPENING ANTIPHONS

~ ‡ ~

~ At Any Time of Year

Celebrant: Blessed be God,
who gave us breath and life.

People: Blessed be God,
who loves us always.

Celebrant: Blessed be God,
who makes us a holy people.

People: Blessed be God,
now and always. Amen.

~ During Advent

Celebrant: Give thanks to God,
for whom we long.

People: Give praise to God,
whose covenant is everlasting.

~ During Christmas

Celebrant: Blessed be God, who has come among us to dwell.

People: Blessed be God Immanuel.

~ During Epiphany

Celebrant: Blessings to God,
who gives hope in the darkness of our lives.

People: Blessings to Jesus Christ,
who reveals God's love unto the world.

Celebrant: Blessings to the Holy Spirit,
who empowers us to be a light for others.

People: Blessings, honor, and glory to God,
today and forever. Amen.

~ During Lent

Celebrant: Praise and thanks to God,
who forgives our sins.

People: Praise and thanksgiving
for God's mercy and love.

~ At the Easter Vigil

Celebrant: Alleluia!
This is the night
for rejoicing and gladness!

People: God is triumphant over death;
therefore shall we rejoice! Alleluia!

~ During Easter

Celebrant: Alleluia! Christ is risen!

People: Christ is here! Alleluia!

~ During Pentecost

Celebrant: Glory to God,
the source of life.

People: Glory to God,
who has breathed upon us.

～ **For Other Occasions**

Celebrant: Alleluia!
God is in the midst of us.

People: Therefore shall we rejoice and give thanks.
Alleluia! Alleluia! Amen.

— or —

Celebrant: Give praise and thanks to God.

People: Let the whole world rejoice in God's goodness.

— or —

Celebrant: Blessed be God,
who makes all things new.

People: Blessed be God's reign,
now and forever.

— or —

Celebrant: Blessed be God,
our Creator, Redeemer, and Sanctifier.

People: Blessed be God's reign,
now and forever.

— or —

Celebrant: Sing unto God a new song.

People: We lift our hearts in praise.

Celebrant: Sing unto God who transforms our lives.

People: Who makes all things new.

Together: Glory to God now and forever.
Glory to God. Alleluia! Amen.

— or —

Celebrant: Alleluia! The Lord our God is one.

People: We shall love God with all our heart, mind, body, and soul.

Celebrant: Glory to God!

People: Alleluia! Amen.

— or —

Celebrant:	Bless God, who has given us life.
People:	Bless God, who has delivered us through Jesus Christ.
Celebrant:	Bless God, who makes all things new by the power of the Holy Spirit.
People:	Glory to God! Alleluia! Amen.

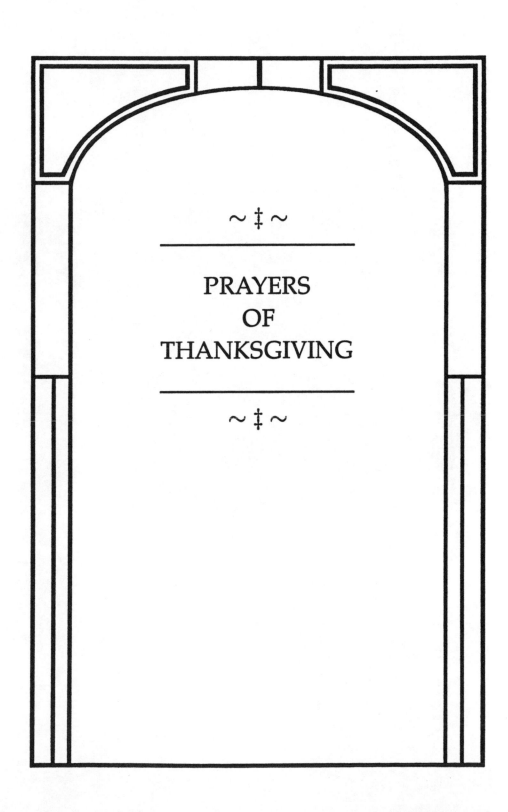

~ ‡ ~

—————————

PRAYERS
OF
THANKSGIVING

—————————

~ ‡ ~

~ Prayer of Thanksgiving

God of all blessings,
source of all life,
giver of all grace:

We thank you for the gift of life:
for the breath
that sustains life,
for the food of this earth
that nurtures life,
for the love of family and friends
without which there would be no life.

We thank you for the mystery of creation:
for the beauty
that the eye can see,
for the joy
that the ear may hear,
for the unknown
that we cannot behold filling the universe with wonder,
for the expanse of space
that draws us beyond the definitions of our selves.

We thank you for setting us in communities:
for families
who nurture our becoming,
for friends
who love us by choice,
for companions at work,
who share our burdens and daily tasks,
for strangers
who welcome us into their midst,
for people from other lands
who call us to grow in understanding,
for children
who lighten our moments with delight,
for the unborn,
who offer us hope for the future.

We thank you for this day:
for life
and one more day to love,
for opportunity
and one more day to work for justice and peace,
for neighbors

and one more person to love
and by whom to be loved,
for your grace
and one more experience of your presence,
for your promise:
to be with us,
to be our God,
and to give salvation.

For these, and all blessings,
we give you thanks, eternal, loving God,
through Jesus Christ we pray. Amen.

~ Prayer of Thanksgiving for Creation

We give you praise and thanks,
    O God of creation,
    for the beauty of this world
    that you have made:

For the healing waters of life,
    which bring us pleasure, health,
    cleanliness, and life.

For the richness of the earth,
    which brings forth fruit and grain for food,
    and flowers and trees to delight our soul.

For the birds of the air,
    which bring music into our days
    and lift our hearts with their flight.

For the animals of nature,
    which provide companionship,
    protection, and labor.

For the mystery and light of fire,
    which gives warmth and heat in the cold,
    and makes our food edible and tasty.

For the sunlight of day,
    which provides direction and opportunity,
    lest we stumble and fall, unable to find our way.

For the mystery of the night,
    the wonder of the stars,
    the challenges of the unknown in the universe.

For the companionship and love of humankind:
    families, friends, and neighbors,
    who give meaning to our living.

We give thanks to you, O God of creation:
    for all creatures, great and small,
    for all mysteries and wonders of this world.

For these, and for all the blessings of our life,
    may your holy name be praised.
    Amen.

~ Prayers of Thanksgiving for Life

Mother of the world,
to you we sing
praise and adoration
for life's abundance
and grace.
You provide for our needs
with the bounty of your womb.
You bless us with the touch
of your breath upon our souls.
You caress us with your love
in our hearts.
Praise and thanksgiving
to you we raise,
with joyful hearts
and grateful praise.
Amen.

This prayer may be read line by line by sixteen different people; it may be read responsively or antiphonally by line; or it may be read by one person throughout.

Thank you for the joy of living.
Thank you for the blessing of love.
Thank you for the comfort of friendship.
Thank you for the kindness of strangers.
Thank you for the freedom to make choices.
Thank you for the wonderment of opportunity.
Thank you for excitement of challenges.
Thank you for the wisdom learned in failures.
Thank you for new beginnings.
Thank you for fulfilled endings.

Thank you for the dawn of day.
Thank you for the peace of night.
Thank you for the re-creation of play.
Thank you for the commitment of work.
Thank you for life and all it brings.
Thank you God for these and all your gifts.
Amen.

~ Prayers of Thanksgiving for Women

Blessed are you, O God, for the gift of life you have bestowed upon your children.

We thank you for the mothers of this world who nurture their children to adulthood with patience, love, and understanding. We thank you for the comfort they give in times of pain and sorrow, for the hope they bring through their sustaining faith, and for the encouragement they offer as they seek new life for their beloved children.

We thank you for the faithfulness of women who live in the covenant of marriage, upholding a model of love and fidelity to this broken and torn world. We thank you for their fulfillment as partner to their spouse, working together as a team to proclaim your love through their love for one another.

We thank you for the women who have raised a family alone as single parents, for their courage and strength to face each new day with its challenges and opportunities. We thank you for the nurture they pour upon their children as they struggle to earn a living and to raise a family with limited resources and hours in each day.

We thank you for the women who face each day alone without spouse, children, or family, for their bravery in creating life, for their formation of extended families, and for the gifts they share with others through their living.

We thank you for the women who have faced the hard reality that love can die and who have engaged the painful rite of separation and divorce, for their vision of a new life and their desire of a realized love.

We thank you for the women who provide love and nurture for one another. We thank you for the hope they express as they seek love and comfort from each other and for their willingness to stand for what they believe.

Bless the women of this earth, O God, the Mother of all. Bless them in their loving and in their working, in their waking and in their sleeping, in their stress and in their celebrations. Bring them to the joys of the promises you have made unto your people; in Christ's name we pray. Amen.

~ Prayers of Thanksgiving for Men

Blessed are you, O God, for the gift of life you have bestowed upon your people.

We thank you for the fathers of this world who care for their children's well-being and safety. We thank you for the protection they seek to provide, the vision they desire to impart, and their hope for a good future for their children.

We thank you for the faithfulness of men who live in the covenant of marriage, upholding a model of love and fidelity in this broken and torn world. We thank you for the partnership they strive to create with their spouse in the large and small tasks of living as one.

We thank you for the men who raise their children alone as single parents, for their willingness to face the stress and strains of daily life with too little time and energy. We thank you for the love they give to their children and for the joy and wonder they impart.

We thank you for the men who face each day alone without spouse or children, for their courage to build a life of meaning and value, for their building of supportive friendships, and for the talents they share to make this a better world in which to live.

We thank you for the men who have faced the end of love through divorce and death, for their hope for new beginnings while living through the pain.

We thank you for the men who provide love and companionship to one another, for their strength to hold fast to their beliefs in the face of opposition, and for their faithfulness to each other.

Bless the men of this earth, O God, the Father of all. Bless them in their loving and in their working, in their waking and in their sleeping, in their stress and in their celebrations. Bring them to the joys of the promises you have made unto your people; in Christ's name we pray. Amen.

~ Prayers of Thanksgiving for Children

Blessed are you, O God, for the gift of life you have bestowed upon your children.

We thank you for the children of this world, for the hope, joy, laughter, and love they bring to life. We thank you for the optimism and wonder with which they face the new day.

We thank you for their delight in little things: a funny sound, a silly bird, a floppy litter of newborn puppies, a simple song, or a giggling friend.

We thank you for their love: their open smiles, their warm hugs, their quickness to forgive, their delight in greeting, the excitement of expectation, and the shy moments of wonder and uncertainty.

We thank you for their eagerness to discover: the sound of little feet learning to walk, the concentration focused on a newly unearthed task, the lilt of the voice using big words, and the boundless energy to be spent.

We thank you for the hope they bring: new life in the midst of tired days, fresh ideas and unimagined ways, the promise of tomorrow, and the fulfillment of new possibilities and dreams.

Bless the children of the earth, O God of love. Bless them when they are lonely or afraid, when they are hungry or full, when they are laughing or crying. Bring them peace, security, shelter, food, and all the necessities of this life. Grant to them the nurture and love to grow to the fullness of their talents and skills. Give them hope for their days ahead and ever surround them with your love; in Christ's name we pray. Amen.

~ Prayer in Thanksgiving for Wonder

We thank you, glorious and gracious God,
for the gift of wonder:
for the joy to be found
in the tides rolling in and out,
a single flower in bloom in a meadow,
for seaweed clinging to the rocks
or floating free;
for a cool, gentle breeze against the cheek,
for clouds drifting past,
for birds floating on air currents high,
for raspberries ripening on the bush,
for grasses blowing and reflecting the sun,

for the stillness of the morning,
for the glory of summer sunsets.
For these and the many wonders of your creation
we give you thanks, O ever-creating God.
Amen.

~ Prayer in Thanksgiving for Surprises

For a friend's unexpected call,
for a letter unforeseen,
for the sunlight bursting thick clouds,
for a porpoise frolicking in the water,
for seals basking in the sun,
for an invitation to dinner on a lonely eve,
for a request to "come along";
for all the wonderful surprises of life
we give you thanks, O God of joy. Amen.

~ Prayer in Thanksgiving
for Inspiration

O God, the author of creation,
we thank you for the gift of inspiration:
for opening our eyes to see new possibilities,
for enriching our minds with visions never dreamed,
for guiding us to trust the unconscious's view,
for sounds to tickle and to delight,
for teaching our hearts to receive the unexpected gift.
For these and the many wonders you have wrought
within the secret places of our souls,
we thank you, O God of endless creation. Amen.

~ A Prayer in Thanksgiving for Love

Most loving God,
we thank you for those who love us.
For our parents who have given us life
and who have provided us with protection.
For our teachers and professors
who have guided us to wisdom.
For our friends
who have accepted our faults and failings
and loved us all the same.
For our counselors
who have helped us to see life in depth.
For our families
who have nurtured us with their love.
For strangers who have surprised us with kindness.
For Jesus Christ whose love has set us free.
For your love which is with us forever.
For these and for all the blessings of this life
we give praise and thanks to you,
most loving God of all.
Amen.

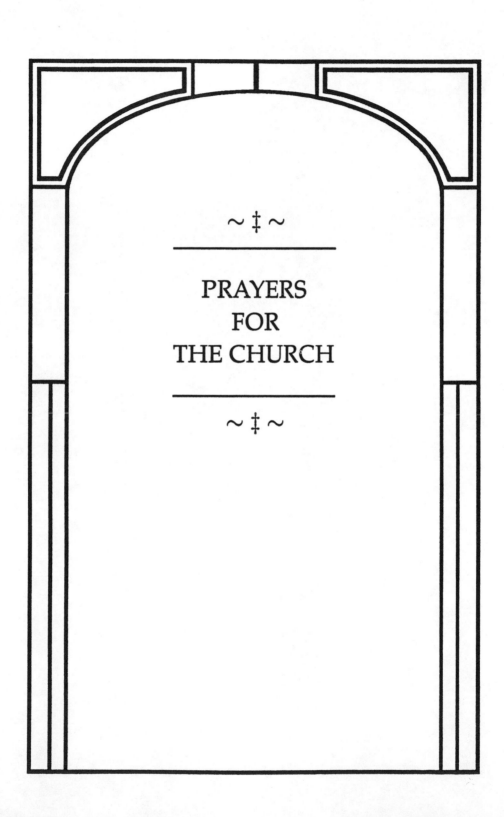

~ ‡ ~

PRAYERS FOR THE CHURCH

~ ‡ ~

～ Litany for the Church

God of Abraham and Sarah,
God of Isaac, Rebecca, and Leah,
God of Jacob and Rachel,
God of our Savior, Jesus Christ,
hear the prayers of your people
for your sacred Body, the Church.

From mistrust in your guiding Spirit.
Deliver us, O God.

From faintness of heart as we learn new ways.
Deliver us, O God.

From the presumption of knowing your Truth.
Deliver us, O God.

From absorption in our institutional affairs.
Deliver us, O God.

From failure to notice the needs of others.
Deliver us, O God.

From the desire to make our own beliefs primary.
Deliver us, O God.

From the sin of dismissing others' thoughts as unworthy.
Deliver us, O God.

From the arrogance of calling another a heretic.
Deliver us, O God.

From division and schism.
Deliver us, O God.

From hardness of heart toward our neighbor.
Deliver us, O God.

From blindness toward our neighbor's need.
Deliver us, O God.

From indifference toward our neighbor.
Deliver us, O God.

From causing our neighbor pain and suffering.
Deliver us, O God.

From provoking death and grief upon our neighbor.
Deliver us, O God.

Turn us unto your ways, and harken to our prayer.
Hear us, O God.

Turn us unto your ways, and lead us by your Spirit.
Hear us, O God.

Turn us unto your ways, and grant us courage to encounter new paths.
Hear us, O God.

Turn us unto your ways, and give us humility in seeking your Truth.
Hear us, O God.

Turn us unto your ways, and send us into the world to proclaim your love.
Hear us, O God.

Turn us unto your ways, and make us mindful of the needs of others.
Hear us, O God.

Turn us unto your ways, and open our hearts to your calling.
Hear us, O God.

Turn us unto your ways, and open our minds to new possibilities.
Hear us, O God.

Turn us unto your ways, and create in us makers of peace.
Hear us, O God.

Turn us unto your ways, and make us lovers of all.
Hear us, O God.

Turn us unto your ways, and open our arms to embrace our neighbor's need.
Hear us, O God.

Turn us unto your ways, and send us into the world as bearers of your grace, mercy, justice, and love.
Hear us, O God.

O God of wisdom and truth.
Harken unto our cry.

O God full of compassion and hope.
Forgive us our sin.

O God of justice, mercy, and love.
Make us witness unto you.

We thank you, most loving God, for the blessings you have given.

For calling us to be your people.
Blessed are you, O God.

For forgiving us our shortcomings, our failures, and our sins.
Blessed are you, O God.

For revealing your love through Jesus Christ.
Blessed are you, O God.

For the gift of life that we possess.
Blessed are you, O God.

For families and friends to nurture and to comfort us.
Blessed are you, O God.

For challenges and opportunities to build new dreams out of past failures.
Blessed are you, O God.

For the wonder and mystery of love.
Blessed are you, O God.

For the salvation of the world and the promise of eternal life.
Blessed are you, O God.

For the call to bear witness to Jesus Christ.
Blessed are you, O God.

For these and all the blessings of this life.
Blessing, honor, and glory are yours,
O God of love.
Glory to you for ever and ever.
Alleluia! Amen.

~ Prayers for the Church

Hear our prayers, most gracious God, for the people of _____
Church. Grant unto them enquiring hearts and minds to seek your Truth
and inspire them to do your will in all that they undertake. Open their
hearts to the concerns of their neighbors that they may seek justice, care
for the afflicted, feed the hungry, and shelter the homeless. May they
be the instrument of your love and grace in this world. Deliver them
from pride, hypocrisy, divisions, and all evil and grant that in their lives
and labors they may praise your holy name, through Jesus Christ our
Savior. Amen.

O God of our salvation,
we pray for your holy, catholic Church.
Where we are divided, heal us.
Where we are faint of heart, embolden us.
Where we are faithful, strengthen us.
Where we have doubts, make us faithful.
In all we do, may your name be praised;
through Jesus Christ. Amen.

Hear our prayer, O God,
for the people, clergy and bishops
of the Church.
Open our hearts to hear your Word
that our lives and labors
may proclaim your love for all.
Bless us with your Holy Spirit
that we may not fear the challenges
that lie before us.
Grant that we may be faithful
until our life's end;
through Jesus Christ, our Savior.
Amen.

～ Prayer for the Lambeth Conference*

Eternal and loving God, we pray to you for the work of the bishops at the
Lambeth Conference. Bless them with the presence of your life-giving
Spirit; open their hearts to the needs of the suffering and oppressed
peoples of this world; remove the barriers that we create that divide us
as your people; Enable each to hear the diverse voices of others; and
grant unto them the abundance of your grace, that your name may be
glorified in all that they do; in Jesus Christ's name we pray. Amen.

---

*This prayer may be adapted for any convention or gathering of the Church.

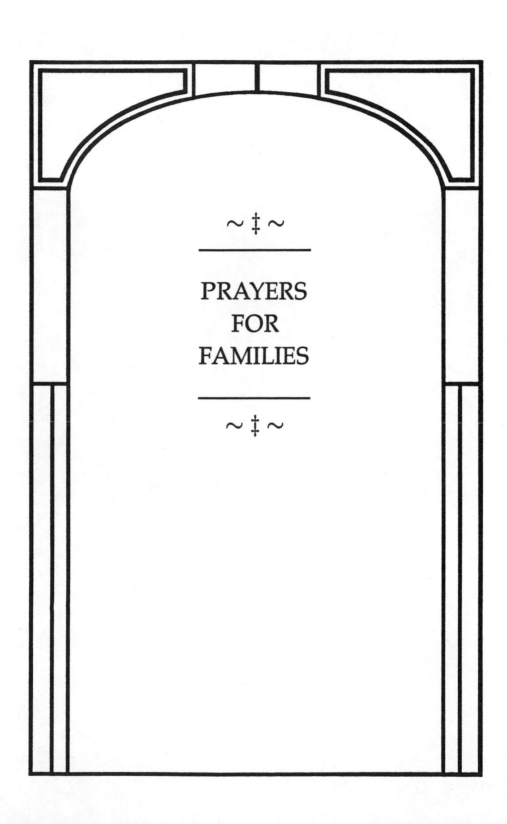

~ ‡ ~
———————

PRAYERS
FOR
FAMILIES

———————
~ ‡ ~

~ A Prayer for a Troubled Family

O God,
there are families
where love
is bought and sold
and treated like a commodity,
a thing,
a power to be wielded
to gain control in another's life;
where forgiveness
is given lip-service
while the offense is held
ever after over the offender's head
like a dangling sword.
How can trustworthiness grow
where no trust is given?
How can love be rekindled
where it has been killed?
You are the source and giver of life,
O God.
Bless the children in homes
without love.
Sustain them,
give them hope,
and people who will love them
and teach them to love;
in the name of Christ who loves.
Amen.

~ A Prayer for Our Family

O Loving God,
bless our family with your love.
Guard us from all danger and harm;
deliver us from anger that leads to division;
empower us to forgive as we have been forgiven;
and send us into the world
to witness to your love and grace;
in the name of Jesus Christ we pray.
Amen.

～ Prayer for Those Who Live Alone

Bless all who live alone, O loving God;
fill their lives with the joy and wonder of love;
let their gifts and talents proclaim your glory
and bring fulfillment to their lives;
in the name of Jesus Christ we pray.
Amen.

～ Prayer for a Divided Family

We are a broken, divided family
of lonely individuals,
each alone;
truly, we're not a family.
Communication with each other
seems impossible,
and love vanishes into the void.
Yet both are what we desperately need.
We all need and want
each other,
but we're too proud to admit it,
or to confess
that we're each to blame
for our separation,
loneliness, and pain.
We add brick upon brick
to the wall that divides
and isolates us.

You alone are our hope,
O God of our salvation.
Your love breaks down
walls that isolate and divide us.
Your love heals, forgives,
and makes us whole again.
Restore us, O God of our salvation.
Reconcile us,
that we may be a family,
and live.
Amen.

~ Prayer of the Heart

Receive the prayers of our hearts,
O God of love.
Let your Spirit
give voice to what we cannot say.
Grant that through these prayers
our hearts and lives may be transformed
to do your will;
in the name of Jesus Christ,
who taught us to pray.
Amen.

~ Prayer for Fathers *and mothers*

O Mother and Father of creation,
we give thanks to you for our fathers *and mothers*
We thank you, and them,
for the nurture, love, and providence
that they have bestowed upon us.
Bless them in their work,
bless them in their leisure,
bless them in the depth of their hearts.
Fill their days with wonder,
their nights with peaceful rest,
and their lives with the presence
of your eternal love;
in Jesus Christ's name we pray.
Amen.

~ Prayer for Mothers

O Mother and Father of creation,
we give thanks to you for our mothers.
We thank you, and them,
for the nurture, love, and providence
which they have bestowed upon us.
Bless them in their work,
bless them in their leisure,
bless them in the depth of their hearts.

Fill their days with wonder,
their nights with peaceful rest,
and their lives with the presence
of your eternal love;
in Jesus Christ's name we pray.
Amen.

~ Prayer for Grandparents

Most loving God,
we ask your blessing
upon our grandparents.
They connect us
with the generations before us
and remind us of our responsibility
to the generations to come
for whom we shall be their ancestors.
Bless our grandparents
with loving families,
with good health,
with compassionate and tender friends.
Grant us the wisdom to give unto them
honor, respect, and love
that their days may be a blessing;
in the name of Christ we pray.
Amen.

~ Prayer for Daughters

We give thanks to you,
loving and gracious God,
for our daughters.
We ask your blessing upon them.
May they never know the injustice
we have known.
May they be emboldened to dream new dreams
and to proclaim their visions.
Grant them your love and protection
as they journey through life.
Enrich their lives with friends,

someone special to love,
a community of faith,
children of their own,
and the challenge of loving and serving
their neighbor
through the use of the unique gifts
you have given each of them.
Grant that their generation
may work for the spread of your reign
where all may live in peace;
in Jesus Christ's name we pray.
Amen.

~ Prayer for Sons

We give thanks to you,
loving and gracious God,
for our sons.
We ask your blessing upon them.
May they never know the injustices
of war, captivity, and oppression.
May they be emboldened
to dream new dreams
and to proclaim their visions
for a better world for all.
Grant them your love and protection
in the trials and temptations of life.
Enrich their lives with deep friendships,
someone special to love,
a community of faith,
children for their inheritance,
and the challenge
of loving and serving your purposes
through the use of the unique gifts
you have given each of them.
Grant that their generation
may work for the spread of your reign
where all may live in peace;
in Jesus Christ's name we pray.
Amen.

~ **Prayer for Sisters**

God of blessing and love,
we thank you for our sisters:
For Mary and Martha
created of one flesh
yet different
in their choices
and in their lives.
You blessed
their sisterhood,
their diversity,
their solidarity.
You blessed them
by your presence,
compassion,
and love.

Teach us to value our sisterhood,
to share our sisters' sorrows and joys,
to trust our own unique gifts,
to cherish our differences.

Heal us by your breath
when we hurt one another,
when we betray one another,
when we deny our love for one another.

Empower us through your birthing
to use our gifts to make a new world
filled with compassion,
grace,
and wholeness,
where none are forgotten,
where sufferings are shared
and joys are proclaimed,
where wars are ended
and love is the basis of our living.

Grant us this
through Jesus Christ
who loved us.
Amen.

～ **Prayer for Brothers**

God of blessing and love,
we thank you for our brothers:
For Peter and Paul,
both apostles
yet radically different.
You blessed
their brotherhood,
their diversity,
their solidarity.
You blessed them
by your presence,
compassion,
and love.

Teach us to value our brotherhood,
to share our brothers' sorrows and joys,
to cherish our differences
and to trust our own unique gifts.

Heal us by your breath
when we hurt one another,
when we betray one another,
when we deny our love for one another.

Empower us through your Holy Spirit
to use our gifts to make a new world
filled with compassion,
peace,
and wholeness,
where none are forgotten,
where sufferings are shared
and joys are proclaimed,
where wars are ended
and love is the basis of our living.

Enable us to work for this
through Jesus Christ
who loved us.
Amen.

~ Prayer for Those Who Abuse Their Children

Dearest Love of God,
she killed *her* child,*
her first born,
her only one.

The screams of the little one
echoed beyond endurance.
Her frustration and helplessness
pushed *her* beyond *her* ability to cope.
She shook, and shook, and shook the child
until there was no more breath
in either of them.
The child died.
She died in *her* heart.

Mother of the world,
redeem *her* from the depth of *her* sin.
Transform the agony of *her* heart
from deathmaker to lifegiver.
Strengthen *her* love
that *she* may once more know the joy of creating life
and the bliss of nurturing the child of your creation.

Lover and Source of all life,
you heard the child's cry;
enable us to hear *her* cry
for compassion and help.
You saw the *mother's* pain;
open our hearts to love *her*
and not be quick to condemn *her*.
Restore the breath of life in *her*.
Renew *her* helpless spirit.
Protect *her* from *her* own sense of unforgiving love.
Grant that *she* may be transformed
and become a *mother* whose love nurtures,
who gives life and hope to the helpless,
as you give blessings to all who ask.

In the name of your beloved,
Jesus Christ, we pray.
Amen.

---

*"He/his" may be substituted for "she/her."

~ Prayer for a Child
Who Has Been Molested

Most loving God,
she has been severely wounded,
hurt beyond words
with the betrayal of trust,
physical violence and abuse,
and the absence of love.
Bless *her*
with the abundance of your love
and with the support of loving people
who will help to heal the wounds,
restore confidence and trust,
and teach *her*
to love again;
in the name of Jesus Christ
we pray.   Amen.

~ Prayers for Women
Who Have Had a Miscarriage

Most loving God,
losing a child is devastating.
Bless all women,
and especially _____,
who have had a miscarriage.
Comfort them in their loss.
Give them hope
for children to come.
Bless them with an abundance of love
that as their bodies heal,
so too may their hearts.
Give them courage to face each new day
in the confidence of your love;
in the name of Jesus Christ we pray.   Amen.

O God of love, source of life,
hear our prayers for _____.
Her baby died before it ever came to birth.
The blessing of your love

was torn from her body,
leaving her empty and devastated.
Comfort her in her sorrow.
Restore her hope for a child to come.
Give her courage and new delight
in the days ahead.
In good time, grant her a new life
that her soul may rejoice
and her body give birth;
in Christ's name we pray. Amen.

∼ Prayers for Children

Blessed God, you have created life to begin with childhood, a time of innocence, laughter, and exploration. Bless, we beseech you, the children of this world. Grant unto them the nurture they need for strong physical growth, keen minds, balanced emotions, and a holy spiritual life. Send unto them teachers to inspire an inquiring and discerning heart, to enable curiosity toward their surroundings, and a knowledge of this global village. Bless them with love, hope, and vision, and keep them ever in your unfailing compassion and protection, for the sake of the one who loved children, Jesus Christ, our Savior. Amen.

O God, the Mother of life, bless the children of this world who are dying from hunger, abuse, neglect, and war. In the midst of their suffering, send your Holy Spirit upon them that they may know the loving embrace of your arms to cradle and to comfort them, to banish all fear from their hearts, and to give them hope for their life. Forgive us the wrong we have done unto the next generation of your children by our indifference, our inaction, and our wrongdoing. Turn us away, O God, our Mother, from sin and death unto life and grace, that your children may live in the fulfillment of your promises; in Christ's name we pray. Amen.

Loving and creative God,
we thank you for the blessings
that children bring into this world:
for their energy and spontaneity,
for their giggles and laughter,
for their creative imagination,
for their sense of freedom and playfulness,
for their love so openly given,
for their ability to make us feel needed,

for their gift of hope for the future.
Bless the children of this world
we pray you:
Endow them with wisdom,
grant unto them peace,
fill their hearts with love,
inspire them by the grace of your Spirit
that they may praise your name
as they seek to create a world
in which their children may live
in the fullness of your shalom;
in the name of Jesus Christ we pray.
Amen.

~ Prayers for Abandoned Children

Mother, God of all,
hear our prayer
for your children
whose mothers
have abandoned them.
Their pain is unimaginable.
Trust has been broken.
Fear and suspicion
govern their inner being.
Grant unto them
that peace
which you alone can give,
the sure and certain knowledge
that your trust is unfailing,
and your love
that makes us all whole;
in the name of your Son,
Jesus Christ,
we pray.
Amen.

I feel I want to punish her
for having left me
when I was so young and helpless.
I hate her with a violence
I dare not speak

lest I act upon it.
Deliver me from vengeance,
O God of love.
Empower me to love
and to lose love, once again;
that I might be free and whole
as you created me to be;
no longer bound in the way
I have become.
For the sake of Christ
who saves.
Amen.

～ Prayers for the Kids on Our Streets Dealing Drugs

Greed and materialism
control their hearts,
drugs control their days,
and hopelessness for a future
controls their choices.
Deliver them, O God,
from the way of evil and death
that our society has produced
as an avenue for getting rich quick.
Empower us to teach our children
to say no to drugs
and yes to the challenges of life.
Inspire the people of this city
to care about our youth,
to protect them from premature death,
and to provide for them
a future with promise and hope.
In Jesus' name, we pray.
Amen.

Our children are bound in slavery
to drugs, money, and death.
Temptation is everywhere:
in their homes where they live,
on the streets where they play,
in their schools where they gather.

Evil surrounds them everywhere
and threatens their lives.
Be merciful unto them, O God,
deliver them.
Deliver them from the bondage
that we have created by our desire
for luxury, ease, and comfort
above all else.
Let not our sins
destroy our children;
in Christ's name we pray.
Amen.

~ Prayer for Children Killing Children

Loving God, our children
are being killed
by other children.
All for the sake of drugs.
We've taught them
to desire gold
and all that money can buy.
Crack
is everywhere;
it's a quick source
of all the promises
television proclaims
as worthy
to possess.
Children buy,
and sell,
and kill.
Help them!
Help us!
Bless us
that we may create
a world of real values,
a world of love,
a world where life
is worthy
and not cheap.
Bless our children,

O loving God,
and grant them life.
For the sake of the One
who called
all children unto him,
Jesus Christ.
Amen.

~ Prayer for Children Going to School

A new adventure awaits them
as they prepare for school.
Excitement for new possibilities
and fear of the unknown
mingle in their hearts.
Thoughts of achievement and failure
slow their footsteps.
Bless all children this day, O God.
Give them inquiring and discerning hearts,
courage to persevere in all they undertake,
the gift of joy and wonder in all things,
laughter and love to share with all,
and sure and certain knowledge
of your unfailing love;
in Christ's name we pray.
Amen.

~ Prayer for Children Leaving Home

It is time to let go,
to stand back and watch
as the young leave home
and go out into the world
on their own.
Bless them, O God,
in all their endeavors,
in their successes and failures.
Guard them from all harm and evil
and make them strong to resist temptation.
Lead them in your paths

that they may be builders of life
and not destroy your creation.
Teach them your ways of justice
that they may care for the well-being of all
and not for their needs alone.
Guide them in their search for truth
that they may praise you in all they do.
Let them trust the love of family
to support them in their time of need,
to care for their hopes and dreams,
and to love them, no matter what comes;
in the name of Jesus Christ I [we] pray.
Amen.

~ Prayer for One
Who Contemplates Suicide

O God of eternal life,
bless all who contemplate
taking their own life.
Grant them peace
from the internal fears and doubts,
from the turmoil of failures,
from the pain and suffering
in their souls.
Endow them with hope
for the days ahead,
courage to make new beginnings,
and love to strengthen
their resolve to live;
in the name of Christ
we pray.
Amen.

～ Prayer for Those
Who Have Committed Suicide

Bless, O God of eternal life,
all who have died
by their own hand.
Grant them peace
from their inner turmoil
and the compassion of your love.
Comfort those who mourn
their loved ones.
Strengthen them
to face the questions and pain,
the guilt and anger,
the irreparable loss.
Help us to reach out in love
to others who prefer death
to the choices of life
and to their families who grieve;
in the name of Jesus Christ
we pray.
Amen.

～ Prayer for Those
Who Hate Their Parents

Mother and Father of this world,
there are children and adults
who have been abused in word or deed
by their parents.
Hatred and anger may linger in their hearts.
Resentment and fear may control their lives.
The ability to trust may have been destroyed.
Protect and comfort those who have been hurt.
Restore to life those who have been damaged.
Make whole those who have been diminished;
through the love of Jesus Christ
we pray. Amen.

~ ‡ ~

PRAYERS
FOR
THE HUMAN FAMILY

~ ‡ ~

~ Prayer for the Human Family

Mother and Father of the world,
we pray for the whole human family.

Many nations are torn by war.
Grant them peace
and healing of their divisions.

Many communities are filled with crime.
Grant them deliverance from fear
and the hope of renewal.

Many families are divided by hate.
Grant them unity
and the blessing of love.

Many children are abandoned and afraid.
Grant them someone who loves them
and the promise of a future.

In the name of Jesus Christ,
who died that we might live,
we pray.
Amen.

~ Prayer for Our Enemies

We pray to you, O God,
the lover of all,
for those whom we have named our enemies.
Deliver us from the hardness of heart
that keeps us locked in confrontation.
Deliver us from the hatred
that binds us in old ways.
Grant unto all people
the blessing of your love.
And grant unto us
such transformation of our lives
that we may make peace with our enemies,
and that together we might make this world
a safer place for all;
in Christ's name, we pray.
Amen.

~ Prayers for Development

A General Prayer

O God, the source of creation, ever-present in the changes of this world, be present with your people who cry to you for help. Empower us with vision and strength to enable the peoples of this earth to acquire the skills and resources necessary to a growing world. Enable those from countries with plenty to share their lives, funds, and resources with those in need. Embolden those with vision to proclaim new ways of creating communities of responsibility. Engage us in learning from one another and in valuing the unique gifts that you have given to the people of every land. Bless your people, O God, who cry to you through Jesus Christ. Amen.

A Prayer for Education

Blessed be your name, O God of our salvation. Look with mercy, we beseech you, upon all who suffer from lack of education. Free them from the bondage of illiteracy by sending teachers into their midst. Give them inquiring and discerning hearts to perceive and to know your truth as well as the skills necessary for life in this world. Bless the teachers with patience, commitment, and devotion to their pupils. And so bring us all to the joys that you have promised unto us, through Jesus Christ, our Savior. Amen.

A Prayer for Food

Creating God, the power of your Spirit hovers over creation from the beginning of time. Bless all who tend the earth to provide food for the nourishment of your children. Bless their labor, their endeavor to feed the hungry, and their concern for your good earth. Where there is drought, provide water; where there is too little seed, teach us to share what we have; where the laborers are few, send new laborers into the field for the harvest. May your name be praised by the tillers of the soil as they plant and harvest the bounty of the earth that you, in your loving compassion, have provided; in Christ's name we pray. Amen.

A Prayer for Employment

Loving God, you made us co-creators in the process of your creation, blessing us with wisdom, reason, creativity, and skill. Bless all who seek meaningful employment that they might provide for the well-being of their families. Let those who have more than they need for life's necessities be moved to use their wealth to create new opportunities for others. Let those who have skills be open to sharing the riches of their knowledge with those who seek the opportunity to learn. Let us all learn from one another, for you have blessed every human being with a gift for the benefit of the common good. And thereby enable us by the power of your Holy Spirit to build up the body of Christ on this earth that your name may be proclaimed and blessed through the good work of all; in Christ's name we pray. Amen.

A Prayer for Water

Creating God, in the beginning your Spirit hovered over the waters of the earth, bringing form to the void, shape to chaos, and life to the creatures of this earth. Bless us with the understanding of the necessity of water for life that we never waste it:

may we cherish its blessing for sustaining us
and give you thanks for life;
may we use it to promote cleanliness
and give you thanks for health;
may we play in it and share our joy with one another
and give you thanks for laughter;
may we remember your great act of liberation
through the waters of the Red Sea
and give you thanks for our freedom;
may we recall Jesus' baptism with sinners
and give you thanks for forgiving us;
may we rejoice in the water of baptism
and give you thanks for eternal life.

Blessed are you, O God, source of the waters of life, source of all blessing; may your name be praised forever for the bounteous gifts you have poured upon us, through Jesus Christ, our Savior. Amen.

~ Prayer for All Who Are Abused

You chose, O loving God,
to enter this world
quietly, humbly, and as an outcast.
Hear our prayers
on behalf of all who are abused:

For children,
who suffer at the hands
of parents whom they trust and love;
for spouses,
beaten and destroyed
by the very one
who promised to love
and to cherish them forever;
for all people
ignored, hated, and cheated,
by the very neighbor
who could be the closest one
to offer your love.

Hear the cry of the oppressed.
Let the fire of your Spirit fill their hearts
with the power of vision, and hope.
Grant to them empowerment to act,
that they may not be passive victims
of violence and hatred.
Fulfill for them the promises you have made,
that their lives may be transformed
and their oppression ended.

Turn the hearts of the oppressor unto you
that their living may be changed
by your forgiving love;
and their abusive actions
and oppressive ways brought to an end.

In the name of Jesus Christ,
who came to liberate the world, we pray.
Through Christ and in us
may your holy name be praised,
this day and forever.
So be it. Amen.

~ Prayer for One Who Has Been Raped

Compassionate God, Mother of all, we beseech you to look with compassion upon all women who have been raped. Bless them with tender friends, with gentle moments of laughter in their lives, and a renewed sense of trust in relationships of love; in Christ's name we pray. Amen.

~ Prayer for Abused Women

Living God, lover of all whom you have created, we lift to you our prayers on behalf of women whose husbands have abused them through word or deed. Grant unto them the courage to leave a destructive relationship, the perseverance to struggle to create a new life, the hope of tender love once again; in the name of Christ who loves and liberates us, we pray. Amen.

~ Prayer for Abused Men

Living God, lover of all whom you have created, we lift to you our prayers on behalf of men whose wives have abused them through word or deed. Grant unto them the courage to leave a destructive relationship, the perseverance to struggle to create a new life, the hope of tender love once again; in the name of Christ who loves and liberates us, we pray. Amen.

~ Prayer for Those Murdered

O God, we pray for those who have been murdered on the streets of our city. We commit to your loving care those who have died, beseeching you to receive their souls into the mercy of your love. Comfort their loved ones who mourn. Enable them to meet the lonely and painful days ahead in the strength of your love. Let the love that you have made known to us in Jesus Christ lead us to create safer streets for all to walk upon; in Christ's name we pray. Amen.

∼ Prayer for Those
Who Live in the Midst of Violence

O God, you created us to live in families where love and gentleness are shared. Bless those whose homes have been shattered by the violence of war, theft, and murder. Bless those who have died that they may rest in your eternal love and protection. Restore unto the survivors the gift of peace, tranquility, and trust that their world may be whole again; in the name of Christ who brought peace into this world, we pray. Amen.

∼ Prayer for Those
Who Face the Dangers of Terrorism

O God of mercy, bless all who live in the face and fear of acts of terrorism. Grant them courage to go about their daily living. Give them hope that one day the hostility will cease. Guard the defenseless, especially the children and the elderly, the infirm and the weak. Bring peace to their homes and faith in their hearts; in Christ's name we pray. Amen.

∼ Prayers for Those
Held Captive by Terrorists

Deliver those held captive, O God, from fear and death. In their days of torture and terror, be near with the power of your love. Sustain them with hope, courage, and trust in your unfailing protection. Grant that they may be returned to the love of their families and to a life of peace; in Christ's name we pray. Amen.

Bless all who are held captive in a foreign land, far away from the closeness of their families and friends. Endow them with strength and courage to face each day. Fill their hearts with the presence of your love, that they may have peace of mind, hope for the future, and the knowledge that they are not forgotten. May their days have meaning, may their nights bring rest, and may their longing for restoration to those whom they love be fulfilled; in the name of Christ, who was captive and who ransomed all, we pray. Amen.

~ Prayer for Terrorists

O God, there are those who suffer and feel the power of injustice so heavily that they resort to acts of terrorism to claim their rights. Turn their hearts from acts of violence against the innocent in search of more peaceful ways to seek their due. Open the hearts of the world that their voices may be heard and their cries for justice fulfilled; in the name of Jesus Christ, the Prince of Peace we pray. Amen.

~ Prayer for Those Who Are Oppressed

Creating God,
you have loved us
since you breathed your breath into us
and gave us life.
Hear the breath of our voices this day
as we cry unto you,
The women of your womb
are weeping.
We are denied
the very life you gave us.
We hunger,
we thirst,
we struggle for life.
Hear our cry unto you;
for here on earth,
we are not heard.
You created us in your image
but we are treated
as less than the dust
from which we are made.
You called us to serve
but our service is rejected and denied.
Bless us;
let us not become hardened,
let us not become cold,
let us not become bitter or cynical.
Keep our hearts soft and pliant,
able to nurture and to love
with compassion and hope.
As you have given unto us,
so let us give unto our neighbor.

Keep us in your image
that we may be lifegivers
even in the midst of death;
that we may be lovers
where there is no love;
that we may be creators of new dreams
where there is no vision.
All this we ask
that your name may be glorified
and your love made known through us;
in Christ's name we pray.
Amen.

~ Prayer for Women

God of our mothers, hear our prayer on behalf of the women witnessing
to your love for all, to the needs of women throughout the world who
seek justice, equality, and peace. Bless them in their witness; inspire them
with love, courage, strength, joy, and patience. Open the hearts of those
who seek to keep women oppressed to recognize and acknowledge the
sin of their acts. Open the hearts of all women to love those who choose
women to be their enemy. Grant that all may see your hand at work in
the world this day. Grant that we may trust in the power of your Holy
Spirit to guide us in all we say and do that your holy name may be
praised; in Christ's name we pray. Amen.

~ Prayer for Widows

Most loving God, you know the pain and sorrow of death; mercifully
hear our prayer for those who mourn the death of their beloved. The
nights are lonely and the days are too long. Comfort them and bring
an end to the days of tears. Bless them and bring an end to their days
of sorrow. Renew them with the joy of life and bring to an end their
days of mourning. Let the bond of love which you have for your people
be the foundation of their hope that love never ends and that precious
moments with our beloved are forever held dear in our hearts; in Jesus'
name we pray. Amen.

~ Prayer for Those
Whose Loved Ones Are Missing

Loving God, the hope and protector of all humankind; bless those whose loved ones are missing. The agony of not knowing whether one is living or dead is a daily torture. The uncertainty of life's future relationships hangs in limbo. Hope rides a roller coaster. Yet each day must be lived. Give unto your people the blessing of your grace that they may face each day with courage and hope. Guard their families from further danger and harm and hold them in the blessing of your love; in Jesus' name we pray. Amen.

~ Prayers for Children

Children Who Are Hungry

O loving and embracing God, Mother of all humankind, we ask your blessing upon all children who are hungry. Grant unto the people of this world the desire to feed, protect, and nurture all whom you have made. Deliver us from the presumption of being satisfied when we have fed our own bellies and neglected the cries of starvation from your children. Forgive us, transform us, empower us, that we may bring food and blessing to all your children; in Christ's name we pray. Amen.

Children Who Are Addicted

Most merciful God, accept our prayers on behalf of the children and teenagers of this world who are addicted to drugs and alcohol. Hear the cries of the parents who are afraid for their children. Awaken the hearts of the parents who are unconcerned for their offsprings' welfare. Empower every community to act to prevent the spread of the use of chemical substances, that the children of this world may receive the inheritance you desire for them: life abundantly. We pray in the name of Jesus Christ who embraced children with love. May we do likewise. Amen.

Children Who Are Dealing Drugs

They are eleven, twelve, and slightly older,
these children on the streets.
Dealing drugs.
It's cool, the thing to do,
the way to be a man,
the way to get all the material things
society has promised and holds dear.
They're too young to have learned
it's also the way to an early death.
Deliver them from the evil
of the system of their lives:
the poverty that makes them feel trapped,
the society that considers them expendable,
the politicians who look the other way
and don't lift a hand to end this sickness;
in the name of Jesus Christ who suffered
and died that we might live.
Amen.

~ Prayer for Friendship

You have blessed us, O God,
with the gift of friendship,
the bonding of persons
in a circle of love.
We thank you for such a blessing:
for friends who love us,
who share our sorrows,
who laugh with us in celebration,
who bear our pain,
who need us as we need them,
who weep as we weep,
who hold us when words fail,
and who give us the freedom
to be ourselves.
Bless our friends with health,
wholeness, life, and love;
in Christ's name we pray.
Amen.

~ Prayer for Friends

You created us to live in community,
O God of love;
bless our friends who provide us
with the grace and love of an extended family.
Endow them with the riches of your blessings:
good health, sight, and mobility,
that they may enjoy the wonders of your creation
and share their delight with others.
Bless them with keen minds and compassionate hearts
that they may create a better life for all.
Guard them from injustice, oppression, and evil
that they may know freedom and hope lifelong.
In their waking and in their sleeping,
in their laughter and in their tears,
surround them with your love
until the end of their days;
and so bring them to eternal life in peace
through Jesus Christ, our Savior.
Amen.

~ Prayers for Those Away from Home

Loving God,
we pray for those
whom we love,
but who are absent from us.
Keep them safe
from all harm, evil, and danger.
Bless them with
peace, laughter,
wisdom, love, and joy.
Grant that we may be reunited
in the fullness of love;
in Christ's name we pray. Amen.

Eternal God,
we thank you for the gift
of love;
for shared joys and tears,
for laughter and hope,

for the wholeness
of being one.
Bless those whom
we hold dear in our hearts.
Protect them from all evil.
Sustain them in time of trouble.
Sanctify them in their work and play.
Through Jesus Christ,
whose love makes us lovers,
we pray.   Amen.

She/he is far away,
lonely and alone.
She is starting a new life
in a city where *she* knows no one
and none notice *her*.
Give *her* courage, O God,
to face each new day,
to find work that gives meaning,
to discover friends who enrich *her* life.
Guard *her* from all danger and harm,
from disease and despair,
and from all which threatens to destroy
the gift of life which you have given
unto *her*.
All this we ask in the name of Christ.   Amen.

~ Prayer for Safety

I/we are afraid to walk the streets.
We are afraid to go outside.
We are afraid of the young men
with guns in their hands,
drugs in their blood,
and death a breath away.
O God,
hear *our* prayer
for families,
neighbors,
and friends.
Deliver *us* from this violence,
from danger and death.

Give *us* courage to face each day
and to walk the streets
in safety
once again;
in Christ's name
we pray. Amen.

~ Prayers for the Homeless

O God, as Naomi and Ruth journeyed from one land to another seeking a
home, we ask your blessing upon all who are homeless in this world. You
promised to your chosen people a land flowing with milk and honey;
so inspire us to desire the accomplishment of your will that we may
work for the settlement of those who are homeless in a place of peace,
protection, and nurture, flowing with opportunity, blessing, and hope;
in Jesus' name we pray. Amen.

Loving Mother and Father of the world,
bless your children who are homeless,
without shelter from the cold,
the wind, the pelting rain, and snow.
Forgive us our callousness
and hardness of heart.
Stir our conscience
that we may redress this wrong
and provide homes that are
both havens and blessings
for those who suffer
as a result of our neglect.
We pray in the name of Jesus Christ,
who came into this world homeless. Amen.

~ Prayers for Those Living in Shelters

Have mercy, most loving God,
for there is no one to feed us.
Protect us, gracious God,
for there is no one to clothe us.
Be present, gentle God,
for there is no one to hear us.

Rouse the indifferent, righteous God,
lest we are forgotten.
Call forth the powerful, almighty God,
lest we go under and be seen no more.
Bring forth a defender, delivering God,
lest we die.
We are your people,
hear our cry.
We are your children,
be our savior.
We are your chosen,
and you are our God.
Blessed is your name forever.
Amen.

A shelter is a place of protection,
not a place to rob one of hope.
A shelter is a momentary respite,
not a place to stagnate, forgotten.
A shelter is a wayside toward home,
not a dead-end street going nowhere.
Teach us to create new life,
new dreams,
new opportunities
for all who live in shelters
that your reign may be known
and your name be praised,
O God who sees and hears
the cry of the homeless,
who knows each by name;
in the name of Jesus Christ,
who was homeless at birth, we pray.
Amen.

Gracious God,
the children are hungry,
they are falling behind in school,
and are ravenous for love.
Grant that we may see their need,
hear their cries, and respond with your tender love;
in the name of Jesus Christ who loved children.
Amen.

~ Prayers for Those in Need

Nurturing God,
we beg your forgiveness
for the starvation of our children,
for the lack of education we have provided
for their future;
for the callousness with which
we have sought our own well-being and luxury
while forgetting and ignoring
the needs of the next generation of this earth.
Turn our hearts to you
that we might change our ways,
acknowledge your forgiveness and love,
and commit ourselves this day
to creating a compassionate world
in the image of your reign;
in the love of Christ we pray. Amen.

O God of life,
you created this world with abundance,
with enough resources
to feed, clothe, and house all people.
Grant to us the will to share
the blessings we have inherited:
the food of our table
with those who are starving,
the materials of our labor
with those who are naked,
the intellect and creativity of our minds
with those who face hard challenges alone,
the natural resources of this world
with those who are in need.
Teach us to understand the world
as one global village,
our neighbors as our sisters and our brothers.
Let your love fill us with compassion
and enable us to know
that we are not benefactors
but recipients of your grace
every time we open our hand
to walk with someone else
through the journey of life;
in Christ's name we pray. Amen.

~ Prayers for Those Abused by Drugs

Our children are dying;
they are killing each other;
daily another child is killed,
gunned down in the street;
and all for drugs and money.
O God, they're babies;
their lives are ended too soon.
They are caught in a vicious web
of our making.
We have taught them to love gold
more than your gift of life,
to seek a quick high
rather than your truth.
Help us; help us all
to end this slaughter of our youth;
in the name of Christ, we pray. Amen.

Most loving God,
we ask your blessing upon all
who suffer from addiction.
Strengthen them to reach out for help.
Enable them to take the first step to recovery.
Bless them with the persistence to persevere
in the fight to be free.
Give courage and hope to their families,
drawing them close together
in the power of your love,
which alone can transform our living;
in the name of Christ who loves us we pray. Amen.

We pray, O God of hope,
for all families
whose lives are torn and disrupted
by drugs and alcohol.
Enable them to identify the illness.
Strengthen them to seek help.
Bless them with the power of your love,
which imparts transformation and wholeness
to those who trust in your name.
Grant that as they walk this tortured road,
they may journey together
and bound close in the bond of love;
in the name of Jesus Christ we pray. Amen.

~ Prayers in a Time to Take Risks

Mary,
you heard a voice.
You answered, "Yes,"
risking shame and disgrace,
ridicule and rejection.
Still, you said, "Yes."
Yes, to the promise
you received from God.
Yes, to the birth
of a firstborn son.
Let your trust
be our inspiration,
your faith
be our guide,
your hope
our course for courage.
This we ask
in the name of the child
you bore,
the Savior of the world,
who came
through God's abiding love
and your spoken word.
Yes.
So be it.
Amen.

O God,
you call us from our settled ways,
out of old habits and rutted traditions.
You call us into the land of promise,
to new life and new possibilities.
Make us strong to travel the road ahead.
Deliver us from false security and comfort,
desire for ease and uninvolved days.
Let your Word and Spirit dwell in us
that your will may be fulfilled in us
for the well-being and shalom of all;
in the name of Jesus Christ, we pray.
Amen.

~

God of creation,
hear our prayer.
The challenges
to make the world
a new and better place
to live
are oft overwhelming.
We feel helpless and afraid.
Inflame our hearts
with the desire
to do your will.
Kindle us with the passion
of your Holy Spirit
that we may step boldly
to the call before us.
In our work and service
may your holy name be praised,
through Jesus Christ
who came to serve
and to transform the world. Amen.

~

How easy it is
to ignore the world,
to hide in our own backyard
and tend our private needs.
How easy it is
to pretend not to see,
to want comfort and peace.
How easy it is
to lie to ourselves
and say, "All's fine.
No need to get involved.
I can't make a difference anyway."
Call us from such indifference,
complacency, and coldness of heart.
Disturb our souls that we may live
to serve those hungry, illiterate, and homeless,
those orphaned, widowed, and oppressed,
those sick, suffering, and dying.
In serving them, may we come to know
the meaning of loving you;
in the name of Jesus Christ, we pray. Amen.

～ Prayers for Those Who Are Afraid

The unknown is terrifying,
responsibility is overwhelming,
the untapped anger cannot be born.
Hear our cry, O God of love,
for all so trapped in fear.
Open our hearts to trust
your presence to guide us
in the unknown places;
teach us to know
you will support us in all
that we undertake;
free us to share with you
the rage within, knowing
you will never desert us;
in the name of Jesus Christ
who understood our fears,
we cry our prayer. Amen.

We have been hurt so deeply
we cannot trust.
We cannot love or hate.
All feelings have been replaced
by a cold detachment.
Never will we allow
such searing pain again.
Lead us from this unutterable sorrow.
Lead us to an open heart.
Lead us to the place
where fear does not control us.
For the sake of Jesus Christ
who came to give life abundantly. Amen.

～ Prayer for Those Seeking Meaning

Eternal Wisdom,
source of life and grace,
bless all who are seeking
the meaning of this life.
Endow them with courage
to risk the unknown.

Bless them with wonder
to be still and rejoice.
Anoint them with wisdom
to understand the potential
of their dreams.
Blessed is your name,
now and evermore. Amen.

~ Prayer for the Brokenhearted

O God,
whose love restores
the brokenhearted of this world:
pour out your love,
we beseech you,
upon those who feel
lonely, abandoned, or unloved.
Strengthen their hope
to meet the days ahead;
give them the courage
to form new life-giving relationships;
and bless them with the joy
of your eternal presence.
This we ask in the name of Jesus Christ. Amen.

~ Prayer for Those in Need of Respect

Most merciful God,
there are many in this city
who hate themselves,
who consider their lives worthless,
who have not known the healing of love.
Touch them with the wonder and power
of your transforming love
that their lives may be made whole,
that they may find fulfillment in life,
that they may rejoice in your blessing;
in the name of Christ,
who came that we might have life abundantly. Amen.

~ Prayer for Those Who Despair of Living

Send your life-giving Spirit
upon those who despair of living,
O generous and loving God.
If it is your will,
let them find rest from their labors
that they may have peace.
If there is a call they have not heard,
open their eyes and ears to know it
that they may find the joy of abundant life.
Grant them your blessing this day
and every day.
In the love of Christ we pray.
Amen.

~ Prayer for Those Learning to Be Single

Creating God,
you brought forth life
from nothing and chaos;
bless those who are seeking
to create life
without the benefit of family.
As they arise each day,
stir their imagination and will
to envision and fulfill
a day of hope, love, meaning, and joy.
May their energies be used
to create good for all,
their love be a source
of blessing for others,
their quiet be a time
of reflection
in the blessing of your grace;
through Jesus Christ.
Amen.

~ Prayer for Those Living Alone

Teach us, O God,
the difference between
being alone and loneliness.
May our solitariness
be a way of pain
that enables empathy
for others' needs to grow.
May our loneliness
open our hearts to include
others in our living.
May our aloneness lead
us into your divine presence.
Bring us to stillness
where we may know you are God
and discover the joy of life. Amen.

~ Prayer for Lonely People

Loving God,
there are times in each life
when there is no one.
No one with whom to share
a word,
a laugh,
a sad remembrance,
a gentle touch,
a fond embrace,
a kiss of love.
Bless each who suffers
from such loneliness.
Enrich life with a friend
or gentle stranger
who will spend a moment
noticing
and loving.
In those times
your love shines through,
the world is reborn,
and Christ is known.
So be it! Amen.

～ **Prayer for Those Who Are Suicidal**

Most loving and forgiving God,
hear our prayers for all
who seek to end their life
by their own hand.
The despair is too great,
the loneliness unbearable,
the inability to share
thoughts and feelings overwhelming,
the seeming lack of options a dead end.
Bless them with the strength of love
to meet each day with new courage;
friendships to bring moments of joy
in their days of anguish;
and hope for the future
through the love of Jesus Christ;
in the name of Christ we pray.
Amen.

～ **Prayer for Artists**

Bless the creators, O God of creation,
who by their gifts make the world
a more joyful and beautiful realm.
Through their labors
they teach us to see more clearly
the truth around us.
In their inspiration
they call forth wonder and awe
in our own living.
In their hope and vision
they remind us
that life is holy.
Bless all who create in your image,
O God of creation.
Pour your Spirit upon them
that their hearts may sing
and their works be fulfilling;
in the name of Christ, we pray.
Amen.

~ Prayer for Dreamers

We pray for the dreamers of this life, O God,
for those persons who image new possibilities,
who long for what others cannot perceive,
who spin dreams of wonder and majesty in their minds.
Defend them from ridicule and harsh criticism,
from self-doubt and lack of faith in their dreams,
and from abandonment of this call to make things new.
Grant that from their dreams
may come forth blessings for all humankind
to enrich the quality of life
and the wonderment of us all;
in Christ's name we pray.
Amen.

~ Prayer for Claiming Our Creativity

So many of us think we aren't creative;
yet you made us in your image,
O God of creation.
Teach us to know and to trust
that the dreams we have,
the hopes we dare call our own,
the imagination we daily use
are reflections and sparks
of the creativity you have given to all.
Inspire us to use these gifts
in thanksgiving for the gift of life;
in Christ's name we pray.
Amen.

~ ‡ ~

PRAYERS
FOR
THOSE WHO ARE SICK

~ ‡ ~

~ Prayer for One Who Is Ill

I ask your blessing,
O God of love,
upon my *mother/father*
who is ill.
Deliver *her*
from the confinement
of *her* infirmity.
Strengthen *her* resolve
to live.
Grant *her* patience
during *her* affliction.
Bless *her* with a concern
for the well-being of others.
Restore *her*, if it is your will
to health, activity, and wholeness;
for the sake of Jesus Christ.
Amen.

~

Her eyes open wide,
trusting, hurting,
not comprehending
the pain so new.
Deliver *her* from illness,
O loving God.
Restore *her* laughter, hope, and delight
in running, playing,
and sharing life.
Let not this infirmity
destroy *her* spirit.
Keep *her* safe in the arms
of your love;
in the name of Jesus Christ.
Amen.

~

She has had one disaster after another:
her spouse has left
and *she's* angry over the divorce;
she turned forty last week

and feels life has ended;
cancer has invaded *her* body
and hope has fled away;
there are no children
and *her* sense of immortality has vanished.
Restore *her* to life, O God of hope.
Make *her* whole, O God of love.
Grant *her* eternal life this day,
O God of our salvation.
Bless her, now and forever;
in Christ's name we pray.
Amen.

～ Prayer for a Friend with AIDS*

Too soon he has had to leave home.
Too soon indignities are his to bear.
Too soon he will die.
Too soon we shall be parted,
a friendship
only just begun.
He has shown us
the meaning of courage,
the beauty of hope,
the power of love.
He has blessed us
with his laughter,
his living,
his trust in your salvation.
Receive him into your love,
O everliving God.
Bless him with peace
in his dying,
O God of eternal hope.
Grant to him the promised resurrection,
Most Blessed Creator of life;
in Christ's name we pray.
Amen.

Written for Michael, who died in the fall of 1989.

~ Prayer for Persons with AIDS

Hear our prayer, O God of mercy and love,
for all who suffer with AIDS.
Grant unto them tender and loving companions
who will support them in the midst of fear.
Give them hope for each day to come
that every day may be lived with courage and faith.
Bless them with an abundance of your love
that they may live with concern for others
and not be obsessed with their own illness.
Pour upon them the peace and wholeness
which you alone can give;
through Jesus Christ, our Savior,
who came to give us abundant life,
we pray. Amen.

~ Prayer for Those Suffering Trauma

Most merciful God,
bless (_____ and)
all who have suffered trauma
in their lives.
Support them with love
during their time of shock.
Grace them with peace
as they wrestle with the challenges
of each day.
Sustain them in hope
as they prepare for the days ahead;
through Jesus Christ. Amen.

~ Prayer for Those Suffering with Birth Defects

Bless, O loving God,
(_____ and)
all who have suffered
from birth defects.

Grant them courage
to overcome all obstacles
placed in their path.
Endow them with a vision
of the fullness of life
that they may attain.
Give them hope to find the love
that makes life rich;
in the name of Jesus Christ,
we pray.   Amen.

~ Prayer for Those Suffering with Cancer

Bless, O God,
(_____ and)
all who struggle with cancer.
Empower them with hope
for each and every day.
Provide them with loving
and tender care, laughter,
and the support of love.
Grant them
courage when they are afraid,
comfort when they are in pain,
and your blessing
when all else seems hopeless,
that in their fight with illness
they may continue to praise you
and glorify your name;
in Christ's name we pray.   Amen.

~ Prayer for Those with Dementia

Pour your grace, O loving God,
upon (_____ and)
all suffering with dementia.
It is frustrating
not to find a word;
it is fearful
to lose one's memories.

Bless them with patience,
a loving and supportive family,
and days of hope and accomplishment;
in Christ's name we pray. Amen.

~ Prayer for Those Suffering a Stroke

Have mercy, O loving God,
upon (_____ and)
all who have suffered a stroke.
Remove the sudden fear that befalls them.
Endow them with courage in the struggle
to recover what has been lost.
Grant them strength and hope
to envision new days ahead
and a spirit of faith
to take the risk of living fully
once again;
in Jesus' name we pray. Amen.

~ Prayer for Those Suffering from Alzheimer's

O God of love,
hear our prayer
for (_____ and)
all who suffer from Alzheimer's.
In the days of changing memory,
be with them in their fears.
In the days when memory has gone,
bless their families who suffer.
Surround them with tender love
from family, friend, and stranger.
Grant them peace in their hearts,
a secure home environment,
and dignity in their lives.
May each day bring a blessing,
hope, and greater love;
in the name of Christ we pray. Amen.

~ Prayer for Those Having a Hysterectomy

O God, our Mother,
you made us to create life.
Bless (_____ and)
all who face a hysterectomy.
Comfort them in their loss.
Grant them fulfillment
in dreams yet to be born.
Instead of diminishment of body,
let them know enrichment in love.
Where there is pain,
provide healing and comfort.
In the midst of their fears,
give them hope and peace;
in the name of your child,
Jesus Christ, we pray. Amen.

~ Prayer for Those Having a Mastectomy

Loving God,
you created us in your image
and proclaimed good
all that you had made.
Hear our prayer
for (_____ and)
all who face a mastectomy.
Let there be no fear or shame.
Let them know the wholeness
provided by love.
Let them feel beautiful and complete once again;
in the name of Christ we pray. Amen.

~ Prayer for Those Who Have Lost a Part of the Body

Merciful and loving God,
bless (_____ and)
all who have suffered

the loss of a limb,
or been disfigured,
through surgery or an accident.
Bless them
with courage, hope, and faith
to face the trauma
and to start life anew.
Give them
patience in their rehabilitation,
laughter in their days of despair,
and the strength of your love in their need;
in Christ's name we pray. Amen.

~ Prayer for Those in Chronic Pain

O God of love, hear our prayer for those who live with chronic pain. Bless them with your Holy Spirit that they may have the courage and patience to face each day. Give them an abundance of laughter and love to combat the pain. Provide them with tender and compassionate medical care that their burden may be eased. Grant them a spirit of wonder and grace that their lives may be rich with the joy of life; in the name of Jesus Christ who heals, we pray. Amen.

~ Prayer for Those in Acute Pain

Hear our prayer, O God, for those who suffer in pain this day. Deliver them from fear and despair and grant that their trust may be in you to make them whole. Provide them with doctors and nurses who can relieve their pain. Restore them to health and to the joy and love of life; in the name of Jesus Christ who healed the sick. Amen.

~ Prayer for Those Who Fear Pain

Bless all who live in fear of pain, O God of mercy. Teach them to know that they can face with confidence that which they most dread through the power of your love. Lead them through the days of uncertainty and fear that lie ahead and bring them to the peace which you alone can give; in the name of Jesus Christ we pray. Amen.

~ Prayer for Those Dying in Pain

Most loving God, nothing can be done to ease or remove the pain for many who are dying. Our medicines are inadequate, our technology failing. Bring peace to those who suffer so in their last hours of life. Bless them with your abiding presence, that though the pain be great, the joy of your nearness brings comfort and hope. Deliver them from their distress and receive them into the arms of your mercy and love; in Christ's name we pray. Amen.

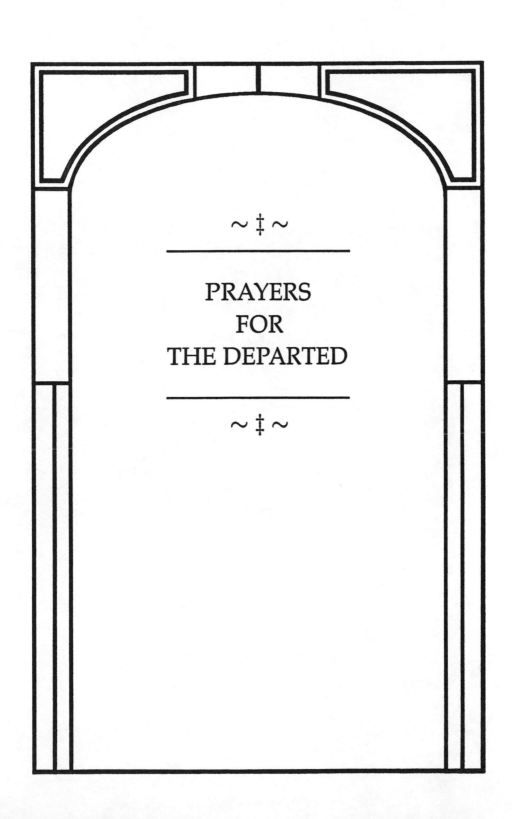

~ ‡ ~

PRAYERS
FOR
THE DEPARTED

~ ‡ ~

~ Vigil with the Dying

Celebrant: God be with you.

People: And also with you.

Celebrant: Lift up your hearts.

People: We give them to God.

Celebrant: Let us pray in the words our Savior, Jesus Christ, has taught us.

The Lord's Prayer in its old or contemporary version may be said.

Celebrant: O God of love and everlasting life,
hear our prayers that we offer
on behalf of _____.
Deliver *her/him* from the power
of sin and death.

People: God of love, hear our prayer.

Celebrant: In your mercy and goodness,
forgive *her* the sin *she* has done,
and grant unto *her* eternal peace.

People: God of love, hear our prayer.

Celebrant: May those good works that *she* has begun
continue in us to bring you glory.

People: God of love, hear our prayer.

Celebrant: May *she* know that *she* shall ever live
in our hearts and memories
and that *her* name shall be remembered.

People: God of love, hear our prayer.

Celebrant: Depart, _____, out of this world,
in the name of God who gave you life,
in the name of Jesus Christ who set you free,
in the name of the Holy Spirit
who sanctifies you forever.
May you rest in peace in God's everlasting love.

People: Amen.

~ Prayer for a Baby Who Died*

She was so small,
so beautiful,
so full of hope and promise.
What a blessing she has been
to all of us who knew her
those few short months.
She taught us to love,
to hope beyond expectation,
to trust in that which is unseen.
She drew us together
in our anxiety,
our moments of despairing and hopelessness,
as well as in our joys and delight,
and in her every breath.
Her life ended prematurely;
just so had she been born.
Too soon she died.
We wept.
The tears continue.
We hugged
and held one another.
The pain will always linger.
Our hearts emptier
for her absence
and the unfulfilled dreams
she promised.
But the love she brought
into our lives will live forever.
Thank you for giving her to us.
Thank you for the blessing
that she will always be.
Thank you for the love we
would never have known,
but for her
and her brief days with us.
Thank you for _____,
our blessed child of grace.
Amen.

---

*Written in memory of Abigail, the firstborn child of friends, who was born three months prematurely and who died five months after her birth.

~ Prayers of One Who Is Dying*

Creator of life,
I am dying.
I feel the energy of life
slipping away.
The breath you gave me is thin.
The body you gave me is wasted.
The health you gave me is gone.
Forgive me
the hours I have wasted,
the loves I have hurt,
the dreams I have ignored.
Forgive me
my doubts,
my lack of trust,
my fear.
You promised me life;
hold me close forever in your love.
You promised me hope;
sustain me now
in the darkness that overwhelms me
and grant me your peace;
in the name of Jesus Christ,
forget me not, I pray.
Amen.

Loving God,
receive my body and soul
unto your care.
Bless me
as I return to the dust
from whence you created me.
Bless me as I enter the paradise
which you promised me.
Bless my family and friends
as I depart from them.
In the name of Jesus Christ,
through whom I have been sealed
and marked as yours forever,
I pray.
Amen.

Written for Fred, who died of cancer.

~ Prayer for Those Dying of Illness

O God of resurrection, who raised Jesus Christ from the dead, we pray to you on behalf of all who are dying this day. May they know the comfort of your presence, the power of your love to give life even in the face of death, and the hope of your salvation. May they be blessed with the presence of family and friends to banish their loneliness and fears, the love of those who care for them to ease their pain, and the hope of always being remembered by those whom they have loved. All this we ask through the one who died for us that we might live, Jesus Christ, our Savior. Amen.

~ Prayer for Those Dying of AIDS

O God of love, whose mercy has always included those whom we have forgotten, those whom we have isolated, and those who suffer, bless we beseech you all who are afflicted with AIDS. Comfort them in their pain, sustain them in their days of hopelessness, and receive them into the arms of your mercy in their dying. Open our hearts to provide for their needs, to take away their isolation, to share their journey of suffering and sorrow, and to be present with them that no one need die alone. Bless those who mourn the death of their friends and lovers that they may not be overwhelmed by death but may receive comfort and strength to meet the days ahead with trust and hope in your goodness and mercy; in Jesus' name we pray. Amen.

~ Prayer for Those Dying Due to War

O God, whose weakness of a despised death is our strength, we pray to you on behalf of all who are dying in the world through war and acts of terrorism. Bless them with your gift of eternal life and comfort their families who mourn. Teach us to find healthy ways to solve our differences in this world; turn our hearts from violence, terrorism, and war. Grant to all the openness to hear the voices of those considered "the enemy"; grant to the powerless the power to articulate their needs; and grant to the strong the willingness to lay down their might that reconciliation and peace may inhabit your creation; in the name of the Prince of Peace we pray. Amen.

~ Prayers for Those Who Have Died in the Hope of Freedom

Most blessed God,
hear our cries for the people of _____ :
the children have been slaughtered,
fear is engendered in every neighborhood,
hope hangs by a thread.
Bless them with courage to face each new day,
strength to continue their struggle for freedom,
and love to nurture them along the way.
We pray in the name of the one
who came to bring liberation, hope, and love
to all humankind,
Jesus Christ our Savior. Amen.

Loving God,
we beseech you to bless
all who have died in the struggle
for freedom and democracy.
May they rest in peace,
having given their lives
for the good of all.
Grant unto those who love them
comfort in their mourning
and a sure and certain hope
in the days ahead;
in Christ's name we pray.
Amen.

Give hope, O God,
to those who witnessed the slaughter
of their friends and neighbors
who fought for freedom and democracy.
Grant repentance and forgiveness to those
who hardened their hearts to kill,
and so transform their lives
that they may do justice,
love mercy, and walk humbly
before you and their neighbor.
Bless the martyrs of _____.
Grant unto them eternal rest,
a place of honor in the hearts
of their nation

and remembrance by all people everywhere
who care for justice, freedom, and peace.
Grant unto us
the courage to follow in their footsteps,
that we may spend our days
and commit our lives
to the liberation of all who are oppressed;
in the name of Jesus Christ, we pray.
Amen.

~ Prayer for Those Who Die at the Hand of Another

Hear our prayers, O God,
for those who die
at the hands of another.
Bless the departed;
grant them life with you.
Bless the murderers;
grant them a new life,
the opportunity to be redeemed,
a second chance.
Bless those who mourn;
grant them peace;
for Jesus Christ's sake we pray.
Amen.

~ Prayer of Mourning

O God of life,
my friend has died.
I miss *her/him*.
I feel as though a part of me is dead as well.
Her laughter's ended.
Her touch is gone.
Her words echo in my ears.
Too soon,
too soon we're parted.
This mortal life is fleet.

Bless *her*
in eternal life.
Bless me
in this daily life.
Unite us in your love
that what we had become together
may continue to grow
and to praise your name;
through Jesus Christ,the first born
who died for us.
Amen.

∼ Prayer for Those Who Mourn

Bless those who mourn, eternal God,
with the comfort of your love
that they may face each new day with hope
and the certainty that nothing can destroy
the good that has been given.
May their memories become joyful,
their days enriched with friendship,
and their lives encircled by your love;
in Christ's name we pray. Amen.

∼ Prayer of a Family Whose Child
  Is Killed in an Accident

Too soon
she/he is gone.

Why couldn't it have been
one of us who are old,
whose dreams are spent,
whose days are numbered?
Why could not we have died instead?

Why *her*?
Why one so young,
so full of promise?

Why?
Comprehension stumbles.
Sanity wavers.
Reason fails.
What then is left?
Trust.

Trust in the goodness and mercy of God.
Trust in Christ's resurrection from the dead.
Trust in the power of God's Spirit
to give us wholeness when we are brokenhearted,
to give us peace when there is none,
to give us life in the face of death.

In the midst of this void
grant us your love, O God.
Fulfill your promises of old:
heal our pain,
comfort our sorrow,
restore our faith,
that we may live;
in Christ's name we pray.
Amen.

∼ Prayers for a Child Killed in an Accident

She/he is the treasure of our lives,
the blessing of our hearts,
the joy of our living.
Now life is ended and death has come.
By the power of your love,
enable us to trust in your goodness and mercy.
Bless _____,
most loving God,
with the hope of resurrection,
the gift of eternal life,
and the anointing of your peace.
May the memories of *her* days
be ours to cherish.
May the good deeds that *she* had begun
be our calling to continue.
May the love that flowed through *her*
now surge in us;

that *her* life may make an impact on this world
until our days have ended
and we rest together in your peace and love.
All this we ask through Jesus Christ our Savior.
Amen.

~

We thank you, O God,
for the life of _____:
for the love that *she* shared so abundantly,
for the warmth of *her* laughter,
for the joy of *her* presence,
for the easy conversation we knew,
for *her* clear articulation of thought and feeling,
for *her* openness and direct way,
for *her* compassion for others,
for the spontaneity of *her* heart,
for the generosity of *her* soul,
for the companionship *she* gave,
for the years we spent together,
for *her* friendship and love,
for the wondrous beauty of *her* life.
For these and all the blessings
that _____ gave to us,
we thank you, O God of love.
Amen.

~ ‡ ~

PRAYERS
FOR
THE WORLD

~ ‡ ~

~ Prayers for the World

I bid your prayers for the people of this world:

(silence)

(During the silences, the people may pray in the silence of their hearts, or may name particular places in the world for whose people they wish to pray.)

I ask you to pray especially for women in their struggle with injustice:

- Women produce nearly half of the world's food supply yet they represent three-quarters of the world's malnourished.

    Pray for those who are hungry.

    (silence)

- Two-thirds of the world's 800 million illiterates are women.

    Pray for those who seek deeper knowledge.

    (silence)

- Only one woman in every one hundred owns land.

    Pray for those who are homeless.

    (silence)

- Sixty percent of the world's refugees are women.

    Pray for those whose homelands are in turmoil.

    (silence)

- In the United States 93 percent of all public assistance recipients are women.

    Pray for those who are powerless.

    (silence)

- Two out of three women in this nation will experience domestic violence during their lives.

    Pray for those who are abused throughout the world.

    (silence)

- On every continent, women strive for justice, nourishment, development, equality, and peace.

    Pray for God's blessing upon all.

    (silence)

I ask you to pray especially for men in their struggle to forsake patriarchy and oppression:

- On every continent, men of power wage war against their brothers.

  Pray for a change of heart that they may seek peace.

  (silence)

- In South Africa, white men lord it over blacks.

  Pray for justice.

  (silence)

- In South America, drug lords make millions while neighbors live in fear and children starve.

  Pray for a compassionate world.

  (silence)

- In the U.S., military men spend billions on weapons to kill while the cost of one instrument of war could house the homeless.

  Pray for eyes to behold our evil and for forgiveness for our sins.

  (silence)

- On every continent, men strive for justice, equality, peace, and the end of oppression.

  Pray for God's blessing upon all.

  (silence)

I ask you to pray especially for children in their need for a future.

- Children are starving.

  Pray that we may feed their bodies, their hopes, and their dreams.

  (silence)

- Children are homeless.

  Pray that we may build them shelters from the cold-heartedness of this world.

  (silence)

- Children are abused.

    Pray that we may give them release from their oppression.

    (silence)

- Children are trapped in the midst of war.

    Pray that we may work for peace in their land.

    (silence)

- Children are taught to hate others not like themselves.

    Pray that we may all learn to love the diversity which God created.

    (silence)

- On every continent, children seek food, shelter, freedom, peace, and love.

    Pray for God's blessing upon all.

    (silence)

~ Prayers for Peace

God of peace,
we beseech your blessing
upon this torn and broken world.
We live in a time of
hate,
mistrust,
fear,
and violence.
Bless us with your Holy Spirit
that we may follow in your ways
and create a world
where all may live in peace.
We ask this in the name of
Jesus Christ
who came into this world
as the Prince of Peace.
Amen.

You have promised unto us
the peace which the world cannot give.
Help us, O God, to seek your peace
above our desire for justification,
above our need for vindication,
above our impulse to war with our neighbor.
Teach us, O God, to love rather than to hate,
to build rather than to destroy,
to nurture peace, hope, and life for all;
in Christ's name we pray.
Amen.

~ Prayer for Ministry

Dear God,
loving God,
source of life,
we pray to you
on behalf of all who are dying
of hunger,
thirst,
and our neglect.
Comfort them.
Change our inaction
to involvement.
Stir us
to become lifegivers,
in your image
as you made us to be;
We pray in the name of Christ,
who called us
to feed the hungry,
clothe the naked,
heal the sick,
release the captive,
and comfort the oppressed.
Amen.

~ Prayers for Justice

Oppression

O God, you created us in your own image: grant us grace to contend against all evil and to make no concession with oppression. Strengthen our resolve to create justice, freedom and peace for all people on earth; in the name of Christ we pray. Amen.

Injustice

Just and loving God, you created us in your image: mercifully grant that we may seek creative, life-giving ways to change the systems of injustice in this world; empower us to transform that which is evil and corrupt, bless us with energy to maintain the struggle for justice for all people, hearten us when the battle wearies us, and unite us in the common cause for equality, justice, and peace; in Jesus Christ's name we pray. Amen.

Compassion

O God, you love us tenderly like a Mother, teach us to have a compassionate and gentle love for one another, to hate only that which is evil and destructive of your children of this earth. Let the milk of your breasts that nourishes us through your Word and Wisdom cleanse our hearts from prejudice, hatred, and oppression; fill our hearts with the passion of your Holy Spirit that we may strive to accomplish your will on earth that all may have life abundantly and live in peace; in Christ's name we pray. Amen.

Liberation

O God, the hope of the powerless, you have chosen as your witnesses those whom the world ignores; grant to us speech that our voices may be heard and your Word of liberation proclaimed, that justice might roll down upon us and all life be blessed through the power of the Chosen One, Jesus Christ, who alone with you and the Holy Spirit is powerful, reigning now and forever. Amen.

Freedom

God of power, ruler of the universe, we beseech you to bless those who suffer from the misuse of power and authority in this world. Particularly do we pray for the people of _____. Strengthen _____ and all those who lead in the struggle for freedom and justice. Comfort all who are imprisoned and separated from those they love. Protect the children from all evil and bless them with an abundance of love that they may have courage and hope to face the days ahead. Let your people know that your presence is ever with them, your love ever sustaining them, and your spirit sanctifying their lives even in the midst of torture. Inspire all peoples of this world to join in the movement for freedom, justice, and equality; let us not rest until your promises are fulfilled; in Jesus Christ's name we pray. Amen.

Justice

O blessed God, giver of peace, ruler of justice, the hope of all people: look with favor upon the world you have made and for which your Chosen One, Jesus Christ, gave his life that all might be reconciled to you and to one another. Bless the people of this tiny planet, that we may live as one family in the peace that you intend for your creation. Give unto the peoples of this earth the will to provide food abundantly that all may eat, the desire to protect and shelter every family, the open hand to enable those left behind by technology to participate fully and with equality in the changes and opportunities of the future. Teach us to seek your justice and to put aside our warring ways. Embolden us to speak out against all evil that oppresses the peoples of this planet. Inspire our hearts by the grace of your Holy Spirit, that we may praise you as we seek to feed the hungry, clothe the naked, visit the sick and imprisoned, and grant release to the captive, as Jesus Christ called us to do; in the name of Christ, we pray. Amen.

~ Prayer for a Nation Divided over War

They died
for the cause
in which their nation believed.
Some opposed the war.
Some went willingly.
Some were drafted without choice.
Some fled to another land.

Men and women were divided.
But those who fought,
did so in hell.
They saw their brothers and sisters die.
They gave their own lives
that others might live.
May we who enjoy life
never forget
the cost of war:
the sacrifice of those who died,
the sorrow of those who mourn,
the scars upon a nation divided.
Heal, O God, our wounds.
Comfort those who mourn.
Bless those who died.
Give unto us all your peace,
which the world and war cannot give;
in the name of Christ we pray.
Amen.

~ Prayer for Those Who Work for Peace

Bless the peacemakers
of this earth, O God of peace.
In their path
there is hope for tomorrow.
Open the hearts of all
to hear their message of shalom
for the world.
You created us as one,
teach us to live as one family.
Empower us to put away our weapons
and the race for power and might.
Teach us to love
as you love us,
with grace and truth;
in the name of the Prince of Peace,
Jesus Christ, we pray.
Amen.

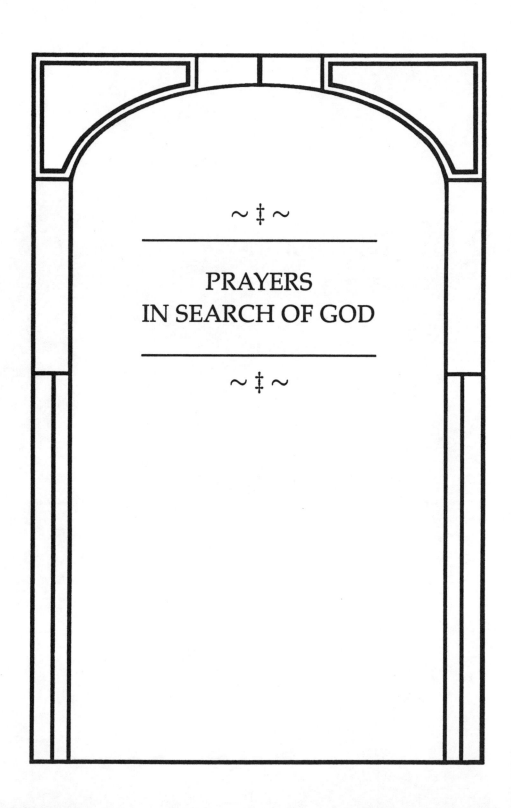

~ ‡ ~

_____

PRAYERS
IN SEARCH OF GOD

_____

~ ‡ ~

~ Prayer to God

How do I name you,
when the words of tradition
speak of oppression,
abuse, and countless tears?
How do I name you,
when the words I seek
seem strange, empty,
and without history or feeling?
How do I name you,
when you are beyond
naming, beyond knowing?
Yet name you I shall;
for you are my heart,
my life, my hope.
I shall name you
"the holy one who
hears my cry,
understands my pain,
and loves me as I am."
To you I pray and give thanks.
So be it.   Amen.

~ Prayer of Doubt

Why am I praying?
To whom am I crying?
What purpose
in my hoping beyond hope?
O One who hears,
O One who sees,
O One who loves,
be here for me.
PLEASE!
Be real.
Be present.
Care.
Hear.
Answer my prayer,
if this be such.   Amen.

~ Prayers When I Can't Pray

I try to pray;
words don't come.
I toss and turn
and feel nothing.
My mind is dry,
my heart is dull,
my soul longs
for life.
Hear my silent cry,
my God, hear me.
Let me not be
a shrivelled reed
or an empty shell.
Breathe on me
and make me whole.
Give me passion
that I may love.
Then shall my tongue praise
your holy name
with words I do not yet know.
So be it.

Mother,
hear my cry.
Inspire my heart
to find words to say
how grateful I am
for life,
for friends,
for work,
for love,
and all the blessings
you have given.
Holy, holy, holy
is your name.
Blessings be yours
forever more.
Amen.

~ Prayer in Lack of Faith

Why is it that
in our hurting and
in our vulnerability,
our humanness is revealed?

Why is it that
when we're composed,
acting so perfect,
so right,
we seem cold as stone?

Why are we touched in our brokenness?
Why do we then feel so beautiful
in all our fragility,
and yet are taught that
vulnerability
is dumb,
stupid,
wrong,
and to be avoided at all costs?

Have we forgotten
how to live?
Have we forgotten
how to love?

O God,
forgive us
when we do!
Amen.

~ A Cry and a Prayer

"Do you have anything you'd like to say?"
"Yes." So much!
So much I'd like
to share
to have confirmed or denied,
to learn,
and to grow,
to understand.
   "Good Lord, deliver us!"

But for now,
that's an impossible dream.
For here,
what is said is not heard;
instead it's
twisted, warped, or distorted.
Words ricochet back
like poisoned darts,
cutting, cruel, and petty,
aimed to hurt or to get even.
Protective walls rise quickly,
gulfs widen,
and stilted images of one another
harden into rigid,
outdated,
but oft-used molds.
    "Good Lord, deliver us!"

Divided
we are falling apart,
slowly dying of our own disease.
Lonely, alone,
needing one another terribly,
we can't see our real need
for love.
Days on end of nothingness,
of going through the motions
of not caring.
If this be so, the end is death.
    "Good Lord, deliver us!"

Help us to care
though we experience
agony and hell;
at least we'll be alive.
Let us not sell short our souls,
not for pride,
nor riches nor gain,
nor politeness,
nor indulgence in another's games.
Teach us to speak words of love.
    "Good Lord, empower us!"
    Amen.

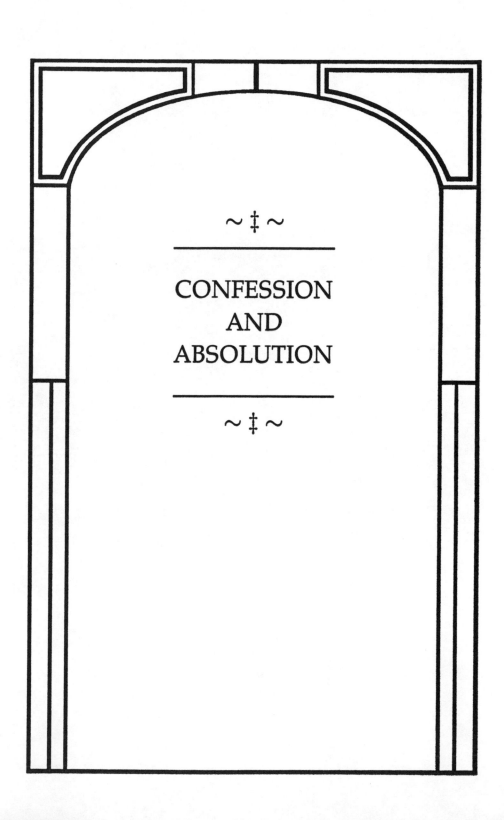

~ ‡ ~

CONFESSION
AND
ABSOLUTION

~ ‡ ~

~ Prayer of Confession

Most loving and gracious God,
forgive us our sins:
those we commit knowingly,
and those we do
without perception
of how we have hurt others.
Open our hearts
to hear your truth,
to understand our failure,
and to reach a new level of wisdom,
that in all we do and say,
we may bring glory to your name
and love and compassion unto our neighbor;
in Christ's name we pray.
Amen.

~ Prayer for a Friend Who Erred

Most gracious God,
hear our prayers
on behalf of our *sister/brother*
who is suffering
from the error of poor judgment.
There is not one of us
who has not erred in this manner
at some time in our own living.
Bless *her*
with new understanding and love
toward *herself*.
Bless us that we might be
supportive and compassionate
bearers of your promises
of forgiveness, hope, and renewal.
This we pray in the name of Jesus Christ,
who came that we might be reconciled
to you and to one another.
Amen.

~ Confession and Absolution

Most merciful God,
we confess to you
and to one another
the sinfulness
of our thoughts,
words,
and actions.
We have betrayed your trust,
we have been less than you created us to be;
we have failed to speak out
against that which is evil,
we have cooperated with systems of injustice;
we have built our prosperity upon the lives
of others who suffer.
We beseech you
to forgive us our sins.
We beseech you
to heal us of our ignorance and blindness.
Open our hearts to your grace
that we may love our neighbor,
strive for justice for all people,
end our wickedness of oppression,
and so praise your holy name,
through Jesus Christ,
our Savior.
Amen.

Absolution

God's grace, mercy, and forgiveness
be upon *us/you*.
God's love fill *our* hearts
that *we* may fulfill the call *we* have been given
to do justice,
love mercy,
and walk humbly before God.
Amen.

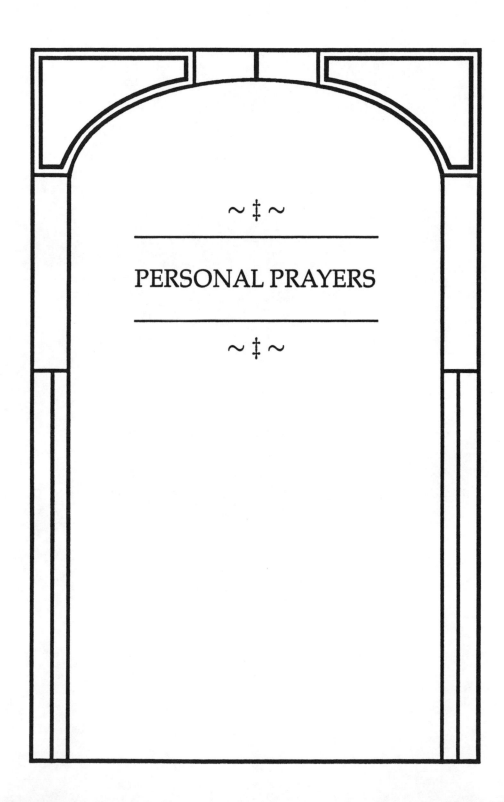

~ ‡ ~

PERSONAL PRAYERS

~ ‡ ~

～ A Prayer of Thanksgiving

You touched me,
O God,
and I received my sight,
and oh,
so much more —
I came alive!

You touched me,
and I saw my hollowness,
the emptiness of my soul,
the death of my life.

You touched me,
and I feel
warm — no longer cold,
soft — no longer brittle,
FULL of love — no longer sterile,
opening — no longer closing,
all because you touched me,
and gave me life!
So be it!
Amen.

～ Prayer for Love

I want someone
with whom I may share my love,
who hears my silent thoughts,
whose arm will support me when I'm tired
and draw me close when I need comfort,
whom I may hold against my breast
to give pleasure and strength to my beloved,
whose children will delight us both,
whose life with mine shall breathe as one.
O God,
hear my prayer,
and grant me my heart's desire.
Amen.

～ A Pregnant Woman's Prayers

I fear
I'm pregnant.
I have no husband.
Whom can I tell?
My parents,
my friends,
my employers?
I haven't the courage
to tell anyone.
The father is away;
I'm alone.
No one with whom
to share
either joy or fear.
No one
for whom
my joy is good news!
To them
my pregnancy
is shocking,
disgusting,
shameful.
O God,
we are so alone,
this holy child and I.
Be near us,
hear us,
protect us,
and grant us both
the gift of life.
Amen.

～

O God,
I'm pregnant!
My heart sings,
my womb is full.
To all the world
I whisper the shout
of my love.
A child is growing,

born of love,
uniting two
who are already one;
becoming new
who through this child
once again are reborn.
Alleluia! Alleluia! Alleluia!
Amen.

~ Prayer for Those Who Have Been Criticized

"What do you know?"
"You'll never make it!"
"You certainly aren't like me."
"You're too young."
"You're not good enough."
"Don't call us, we'll call you."
"You never do anything right."
Loving God,
you are in the midst of life.
Deliver us from the pain
of words that kill the spirit.
Deliver us from saying them to another.
Deliver us from hardness of heart
that blinds us to the death we cause.
Grant that we may follow
the path of Jesus Christ
who spoke words of life,
empowerment, and grace,
for the sake of your Chosen One
who came to save. Amen.

~ Prayer of One Who Feels Rejected

O God, I wasn't counted worthy.
The pain of rejection
is great enough to be denied.
It's so easy to pretend

that it doesn't matter.
But the truth is that it hurts
when others account me of little worth.
Teach me to face the truth.
Teach me to own the hurt
and not to become calloused
toward my own feelings
or those of another.
Teach me to live and to love
in the midst of this pain.
Teach me to learn and to grow
in wisdom, word, and deed,
that your name may be praised
in all that I am;
in Christ's name I pray.
Amen.

~ Prayer of Despair

I have been rejected and despised;
I am hurting and destroyed by the pain.
I am angry with others and with you, O God,
for there is no comfort, none anywhere.
I call your name and you are absent.
I wonder why you let me suffer so.
My cries echo in the universe
and ring in my ears
and I am weary of the taste of my tears.
Hear my plea, O God of love.
Let me not be destroyed
by this agony on the brink of death.
I am like a broken reed,
fragile and crushed.
Hear my plea, O God of love.
Let me not be destroyed.
Amen.

~ Prayers for My Beloved

Far Away

Dearest God,
my beloved
is far away.
He is lonely,
isolated,
and hurting,
away from those whom he loves.
Heal the dark hours of pain;
transform his loneliness
into a renewed and
deeper compassion for others
who have no one to love.
Bless him
with the life-giving joy
of the love
I have for him.
Let my love
be a reminder
of your embracing
and eternal love.
May he make new friends
in this interlude
to bring him laughter,
to share his food,
to enrich his days.
Bring him home
to those he loves
and who love him;
in Christ's name I pray.   Amen.

Alone

Loving God,
my beloved
is alone.
May this time
be for him
a period of renewal,
a breath of life,
a refreshment from stress.

Fill his heart with
love, hope, and fulfillment.
Inspire him in his work,
refresh him in his play,
and grant him peace;
in Christ's name I pray.
Amen.

Dream New Dreams

Creating God,
grant unto my beloved new life.
Heal his wounds;
inflame his imagination;
renew his love.
May he dream new dreams,
know courage unbounding,
and be filled with peace.
All for the glory of your name,
through Jesus Christ.
Amen.

~ Prayer of Thanksgiving

Mother of life,
you created me
in secret in the womb.
You made two families one
in my flesh and bones.
You brought me
to the light of day
and heard my name.
You blessed me with breath,
hope, and possibility.
You gave me the ability
to reason and to dream.
You have fed me
the milk of wisdom
and encompassed me
with compassion and love.
In your blessings,
I have known time and eternity.

May I always praise your holy name.
May I give thanks to you
with my living and my dying breath.
May I return to you
all you have given unto me,
no longer hidden,
but shining in the light
of your love.
In the name of the light
of the world,
Jesus Christ, I pray.
Amen.

~ Prayer for My Father

My *father/mother* is dead;
I can no longer see *his* face
or hear *his* voice.
I have even forgotten the sound of it.
But *he* is always in my heart
and I shall love *him* forever.
Thank you,
O God,
for my *father* who loved me,
who taught me integrity,
honesty, patience, gentleness,
and love.
Blessed are you,
God of the living and the dead.
You hold us forever in your love;
may your name be praised;
in Christ's name I pray.
Amen.

~ Prayer for an Older Mother

Mother/Father of creation,
she gave me life and loved me.
She nurtured me
when I was helpless and small.

She taught me
the things *she* felt I should know.
She encouraged me
as I sought my own path.
She let me go.
Bless *her*
now in *her* loneliness.
Bless *her*
as *she* loses *her* strength.
Bless *her*
when *she* wakes and when *she* sleeps.
That *her* days may be filled
with joy and peace,
with love and thanksgiving,
with honor and fulfillment;
in the name of Christ I pray.
Amen.

∼ Prayer for My Brother

Praise and thanks to you,
O loving God,
for the gift of a brother.
We are very different,
yet he loves me.
We have gone our separate ways,
yet he cares for me.
We have not always spoken,
yet he is there for me
in times of celebration
and in times of trouble.
We are of the same flesh and blood
and are bonded for life.
Bless him in his work and play,
in his children and in his dreams;
in the name of Jesus,
my brother,
I pray.
Amen.

~ Prayer for My Sister

Praise and thanks to you,
O loving God,
for the gift of a sister.
She has shared my laughter,
my sorrows, and my dreams.
She has understood
the secrets of my heart.
Bless her in her work and play,
in her children and in her dreams;
in the name of Jesus I pray.
Amen.

~ Prayer for My Nephew/Niece

He/she is a delight.
He brings me a new joy in my life.
He fills my days with laughter.
He teaches me to look at life in new ways.
He challenges me to grow,
to accept new thoughts,
to try new things.
Bless *him*
in all *he* does,
in all *his* days;
and grant *him*
the gift of eternal life;
in Christ's name I pray.
Amen.

~ Prayers for a Parent Who Is Sick

Most loving God,
my *mother/father* is ill.
Enable *her* to be strong
in both faith and hope
during the time of weakness.
Bless *her* with good humor
in these trying days.

Grant unto *her* the fullness of health
that will permit *her* to return to life
with *her* family and friends
who love *her*.
Accept this prayer
in the name of Jesus Christ
whose love brought healing
to us all. Amen.

~

O God of love,
hear my prayer for my *mother*
whose health is slowly fading.
She's so accustomed to being strong
that the changes are fearful
and confusing to *her*.
May *she* find peace
in the love and support of *her* family,
hope in your promise of salvation,
and courage to face each new day
with patience, forbearance, and humor;
in the name of Jesus Christ, I pray. Amen.

~ Prayer for a Child's Recovery

Hear my prayer, O God,
source of all life.
My child is ill and I am afraid.
She/he is so fragile and young,
so small and vulnerable,
lying in the bed.
Deliver *her* from this sickness.
Let *her* walk and play again.
Make *her* strong and swift,
full of life and laughter once more.
Bless *her* with your love
that *she* may not be afraid
and restore *her* to health,
through Jesus Christ. Amen.

~ Prayer for a Child's Marriage

God of life,
This is *her/his* wedding day.
You gave *her* to me so small,
a delight to behold,
a sign of your love.
Grant to *her* this day
the love to keep *her* vows,
the strength to face hardship,
the courage to endure failure,
the desire for mutual fulfillment,
the love of your presence.
May *she* and *her husband*
grow old together,
secure in their love,
faithful in their covenant,
sharing their love with all,
blessed by your grace;
in Christ's name.
Amen.

~ Prayer of Thanksgiving for a Baby

You have blessed us with the gift of life,
O God of all living.
You have filled our lives with hope and joy,
with wonder and fulfillment.
We praise you and bless you
for this precious gift.
Make us generous and loving parents,
kind and compassionate,
slow to anger and quick to forgive.
Bless our child with your presence
all *her/his* life long.
Defend *her* from all evil and danger,
give *her* wisdom and an enquiring heart,
the gift of joy and wonder,
and keep *her* faithful in your love;
in Christ's name we pray.
Amen.

~ Prayer for a Pregnant Daughter Fearing a Miscarriage

Blessed Mother of all humankind,
hear my prayer for my beloved child.
She and I are both afraid;
shelter us in the love of your heart.
We cherish this child of hers;
nurture it in her womb to full term.
We tremble for the safety of her baby;
hear our cries and soothe our anxieties.
Whatever happens,
let us not become cynical,
nor hard of heart, nor calloused
to the sorrows or joys of others.
May your holy name be praised
through all we say and do.
Amen.

~ Prayer for a Safe Pregnancy

This life you have given us
is so tiny, fragile, and vulnerable,
safe in the womb of flesh and hope,
yet subject to danger and death.
O God of love, creator of life,
hear our prayer.
We want this baby so much.
Please grant this child of ours
a full term of nurture,
the joy and mystery of life,
and the blessing of your love.
Grant us the fulfillment of our dreams,
a baby to cherish and protect,
a child to teach and guide,
a blessing to our family;
in the name of your chosen child,
Jesus Christ,
we pray.
Amen.

~ Prayer of a Woman Who Has Had a Miscarriage

O God of life,
my body is wracked
with emptiness
and the loss of life.
My Baby.
A child so wanted,
desired above all else,
so loved.
Gone.
Not to be.
Never to hold,
forever to love.
Bless us with children,
O God of love.
In Jesus' name I pray.
Amen.

~ Prayer for a Couple Adopting a Child

We have waited so long
for this child of choice.
Bless us
with an abundance of your love
that we may be good parents,
that we may create a home of blessing,
that we may encourage this child
to the fullness of *her/his* potential.
Bless our child, O God.
Give *her* security in our family,
the joy of laughter in our home,
and the courage to face
the challenges ahead.
Let our child know the love
we feel so deeply for *her*,
and let this love be a strength
to confront the opportunities of life;
in Jesus' name we pray.
Amen.

∼ Prayer of a Woman Facing the Choice of an Abortion

Hear my prayer,
O God of love.
I am afraid.
I have a choice to make
which affects not only my life,
but the lives of others.
Do I carry this child
to full term?
Am I capable of being a mother?
What is right?
What is wrong?
I am frightened and confused.
Help me to know what to do.
Grant me wisdom
to make the best choice
for my life
and the life of a child;
in Christ's name I pray.
Amen.

∼ Prayer of a Woman Facing an Abortion

The choice has been made.
One of the hardest of my life.
Bless me as I go forth.
Help me to face the guilt I feel
so that I may not run away from the truth.
Empower me to own the fear in my heart
that I may have compassion
for others who share my pain.
Bless all who support me
with the strength of their love;
in the name of Jesus Christ.
Amen.

~ Prayer of a Woman Facing a Hysterectomy

O God,
they will take out
the center of my body;
my womb will be empty,
sterile, dead.
Hope is diminished,
a part of my future gone.
Take away my fear and trembling.
Restore me to wholeness and to life.
Let me praise you today and tomorrow;
in the name of Christ who makes us whole I pray. Amen.

~ Prayer of a Woman Facing a Mastectomy

Bless me, O God, for I am afraid.
My body will be mutilated,
my breast removed,
my sense of wholeness gone.
Strengthen me for this operation.
Embolden me to face my fears.
Grant me fullness of life once again;
in the name of Christ I pray. Amen.

~ Prayer of Someone Facing an Operation

Tomorrow a knife will pierce my flesh
while I lie in slumber.
It is for my health;
nevertheless, I am afraid.
Honor my fear, O God,
and instill me with courage.
Bless those who tend my body
and grant them the power to heal me
as you make me whole;
in the name of the healer
Christ I pray. Amen.

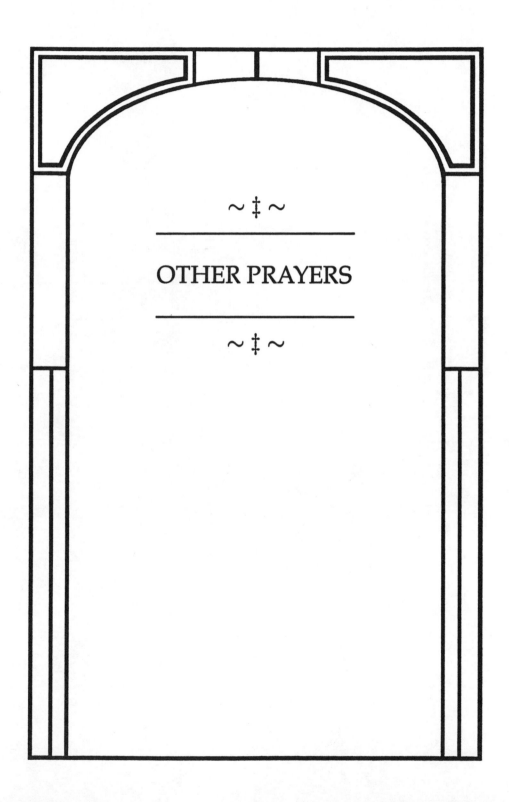

~ ‡ ~

OTHER PRAYERS

~ ‡ ~

~ Prayer for Those in Authority

O God,
to whom all time, space,
power, and authority belong;
grant unto the leaders of this ____ [*nation, city*] ____
the wisdom to govern with justice and mercy,
that your people may live in peace and harmony,
without fear or threat.
Open our hearts to provide
homes for the homeless,
food for the hungry,
rest and protection for the weary,
hope for the poor,
relief for the addicted,
and compassion for the needs of all;
in the name of our Savior, Jesus Christ,
we pray. Amen.

~ Prayer for a Forthcoming Election

Grant unto your people, O God,
the wisdom to choose for office
those who will serve the well-being
of all people given unto their care.
Grant unto those who seek office,
courage to administer justice,
compassion to care for the needy,
a vision for the future
that brings hope to all;
in Christ's name we pray.
Amen.

~ Prayer for a Meeting or Convention

Hear our prayer, O God,
for this gathering of the Church,

_____ .

Grant unto us the wisdom to create
that which is essential for the common good.

Let us not waste time in pettiness
or in fruitless deliberations.
Help us to heal thoughts and feelings
that divide us and fracture your Body.
Endow us with a vision of ministry
that will bless our neighbors
and proclaim your glory;
in Christ's name we pray.
Amen.

~ ‡ ~

LITTLE CHILDREN'S PRAYERS

~ ‡ ~

~ For Mommy and Daddy

God bless Mommy and Daddy.
Keep them safe.
Make them happy.
Let them live to be old.
In Jesus' name I pray.
Amen.

~ For Sisters and Brothers

God bless _____.
Let *her/him/them* grow up strong and healthy.
Keep *her* safe and out of danger.
Teach *her* to share *her* toys with me.
And make me thankful *she* is my *sister*.
In Jesus' name I pray.
Amen.

~ For Grandparents

Thank you God for _____ and _____.
Keep them healthy.
Let them live a long, long time.
Give them happy days
and lots of smiles.
In Jesus' name I pray.
Amen.

~ For Pets

Thank you God for _____, my pet.
She/he is warm and soft and cuddly.
Keep *her* safe from cars
and fleas and ticks.
Make *her* happy in our home.
In Jesus' name I pray.
Amen.

~ For Children Who Are Sick

My friend, _____, is sick.
Make her better.
Take away her pain.
Let her come out and play
real soon.
In Jesus' name I pray.
Amen.

~ For Children Who Are Hungry

There are children,
just like me,
who are hungry.
They have no food.
Bless them with your love.
Send them food.
Teach *me/us* to share my money
so they can eat;
to give up a candy bar
so they can have a piece of bread.
In Jesus' name *I* pray.
Amen.

~ For Children Who Are Homeless

There are children *my/our* age
who have no home.
They are cold in winter
and have no swing or sandbox
in which to play.
Bless them with your love.
Send them help to find a home.
Teach *me* to love them
and to help any way *I* can.
In Jesus' name I pray
Amen.

~ For Children Who Are Lonely

Some kids have no friends.
They are lonely and sad.
Send them friends, dear God.
Teach *me/us* to be a good friend
and to love lonely people.
In Jesus' name *I* pray.
Amen.

~ For Children Who Live with War

Bless, O God,
all children where there's war.
Keep them safe
from bombs and bullets.
Keep their parents safe too
so the children can be loved
when they are afraid.
Help the grown-ups
to stop the war
so the children can live in peace.
In Jesus' name *I/we* pray.
Amen.

~ For Children Who Fight

Some children throw rocks
because they are not free.
Some children are taught to hate.
Teach the grown-ups to love
so children can laugh and play
and be free.
In Jesus' name *I/we* pray.
Amen.

~ For Children Who Live with Hate

Some children are black or brown,
some are yellow, white, or red.
That's how you made us.
Teach us to love each other.
Bless those who are hated
'cause their skin's a different color.
In Jesus' name *I/we* pray.
Amen.

~ For Children Who Have Died

Bless, O God,
all who have died.
Keep them safe.
Let them be happy
and have someone to love.
Bless their families
who miss them and cry.
In Jesus' name *I/we* pray.
Amen.

~ For Me When I'm Sick

I'm sick.
I don't feel good
and I have a fever.
Make me better God,
so I can laugh and play
and go to school
and see my friends.
In Jesus' name I pray.
Amen.

~ For Me When I'm Feeling Unloved

Nobody loves me.
I feel lonely and awful.
I hate myself.
I'm ugly
and nobody loves me.
Help me to know your love,
O God.
Teach me to love
so somebody will love me too.
In Jesus' name I pray.
Amen.

~ For Me When I'm Sad

I'm sad.
I need a hug.
I need to cry.
Bless me, God.
In Jesus' name I pray.
Amen.

~ For a Safe Trip

We're going on a trip.
(Bless Mommy and Daddy
who drive the car.)
Keep us safe.
Let us have a good time,
good weather,
and no fights.
Bless all whom we love
while we're gone.
In Jesus' name I pray.
Amen.

~ For My Best Friend Who Has Moved Away

God bless _____.
She/he has moved to a new town.
She will be lonely.
Send *her* a new friend
so *she* can have fun
and tell secrets.
Keep *her* safe and well.
Let *her* like the new home.
In Jesus' name I pray. Amen.

~ For Me When My Best Friend Has Moved Away

My best friend, _____,
has moved away.
I miss *her/him*.
We had such fun.
Keep us friends
a long, long time.
Help *her* to find a new friend,
and help me have one too.
In Jesus' name I pray.
Amen.

~ Thank You, God

Thank you God,
for Mommy and Daddy,
for all my family who love me,
for friends with whom to play,
for pets who are fun to cuddle,
for the sun and flowers
and all things beautiful,
for each new day,
for surprises and laughter,
and for my life.
Thank you God for everything.
In Jesus' name I pray.
Amen.

~ ‡ ~

CHILDREN'S RITUALS

~ ‡ ~

~ At the Time of Divorce

This ritual needs to occur in a place that is "holy" for the family; that may be in a church, the family's dining room table, or at a favorite outdoor location. It is possible to do this in conjunction with the Ritual for Divorce. The parents make a pledge to the children and give them a gift as a symbol of their vow. The parents may speak in their own words or use the ones below.

Making Vows to the Children

The MOTHER takes the child [children] by the hand or in her arms and says:

I promise that I will love you always whether we are together or apart. I will care about everything that happens to you. I will try to help you feel secure when you are afraid, to give you comfort when you are hurt, and to protect you from all harm.

The MOTHER gives the child a gift, saying:

This gift is a symbol of what I have promised to you. Whenever you see it, remember my love.

The FATHER takes the child by the hand or in his arms and says:

I promise that I will love you always whether we are together or apart. I will care about everything that happens to you. I will try to help you feel secure when you are afraid, to give you comfort when you are hurt, and to protect you from all harm.

The FATHER gives the child a gift, saying:

This gift is a symbol of what I have promised to you. Whenever you see it, remember my love.

Praying Together

The family may kneel together or hold hands as the PARENTS pray:

Bless us, O God, as we who once lived together now are separated and live apart. Bless our children. Keep them safe from all harm, give them courage to face the pain of this division, and the knowledge that our brokenness is not their fault. Help us to keep the promises we made to them; let us not fail them again; in the name of Jesus Christ we pray. Amen.

Blessing the Family

If this ritual is done in a church in the presence of a priest, the priest then offers them a blessing.

Priest: The blessing of God,
                  whose love gives you life,
                  forgives mistakes,
                  and heals brokenness,
                  be with you now and always.

All: Amen.

~ Becoming a New Family

The child, or children, gathers the newly wed couple in the living room or other place of choice. The child performs a ceremony of her [his] own making. Parental help may be necessary to accomplish this, but the words need to be the child's own. For this reason, only an outline is given here.

The People Gather

The children greet each guest whom they have invited and take the guest to the appropriate seat. The children stand at the place of ceremony and the couple comes and stands before them.

One child states the purpose of the gathering:

> *Example:* We have gathered to ask God to bless us as a family.

A prayer may be said.

> *Example:* Bless us, O God,
>   and help us keep
>   the promises we make
>   to be a family.

A Reading from the Bible

A child reads the passage.

> *Possible selections:* Luke 18:15–17 *(Let the children come to me.)*
>
> Psalm 23 *(The Lord is my shepherd.)*

Making Vows as a Family

The children ask the parents questions.

>*Example:* Do you promise to love us?

>*To which each parent in turn answers:* I do.

Each child makes a promise of her [his] own.

>*Example:* I promise to love you Mommy and _____ and to help make us a family.

Prayers and a Blessing

A child invites all to pray.
The Lord's Prayer is said.
A child reads a prayer asking for God's blessing.

>*Example:* Bless us, O God.
>Make us a loving family.
>In Jesus' name we pray.
>Amen.

The peace is exchanged with hugs all around.

Child: The peace of God be with you.

Response: And also with you.

The family then has a party or a meal together with the invited guests.

~ Parent's Remarriage

As Part of the Marriage Ceremony

During the marriage ceremony, the children join the couple at the time of the blessing. They kneel with the parents and the PRIEST says the following prayer:

Bless O God, this new family, especially ____ [*names of the children*] ____. Surround them with love; give them a secure and stable home and a sense of belonging. Protect them from all danger, support them in times of trouble, and give them peace. Grant them the knowledge that _____ and _____'s love for one another includes them in that love and that they are an essential part of this family; in the name of Jesus Christ we pray. Amen.

~ Welcoming a Sibling

Before the baby is born, one of the parents spends time with the child choosing a present for the baby. The gift might be something the baby could use immediately, a rattle, a baby spoon, or a bottle. The child might earn the money to pay for the present so that there is a real sense of ownership in the giving.

The ritual needs to be performed as soon as possible after the infant is brought home.

Receiving the Baby

The child sits in a chair and the baby is placed in the child's lap for her [him] to hold. The child addresses the baby by name and welcomes her [him].

Child: Welcome _____. You are my baby sister [brother]. I promise to love you.

The child may hold the baby and enjoy the moment. When it seems right to the parents, the baby is held by one of the parents and the child presents her gift. If the child is old enough to hold the baby and a gift at the same time, there is no reason for the baby to be removed from the child's lap.

Child: This is my gift of love.

The child should then go with the parents to tuck the baby into the crib. Then the family gathers for a party in the baby's honor; the older child is the celebrant, having been the one who officially welcomed the baby into the family.

~ Burial of a Pet

The children find a box suitable to the size of the pet who has died. It's appropriate to line the box with something soft, a pillow case, a small blanket, a towel, leaves, flowers, or whatever the children select. After the box is prepared and one of the children has placed the pet inside and replaced the top, they gather at the place of burial and dig the hole in the ground. They may take turns doing this.

Song: "All Things Bright and Beautiful"
              "Jesus Loves Me, This I Know"

              Any song of the children's choosing.

Reading: Genesis 1:20–25 *(God created the animals.)*

Burial: *The children place the box in the ground.*

Child: We thank you, God,
              for _____.
              We thank you for *her/his* love.
              We thank you for our days of play.
              Bless *her* now in *her* death.
              Keep *her* safe always;
              in Jesus' name we pray.

All: Amen.

The children may want to place small objects of love in the grave: the pet's toys, a bone, flowers, notes, or drawings. Each child helps to cover the box with dirt until the grave is full. A marker made by the children is placed on the grave. This could be a stone or two sticks tied together in a cross. The grave may be circled with flowers or stones, each child placing one or more of the items as a way personally to say good-bye. Some of the children may want to say good-bye out loud and should be encouraged to do so.

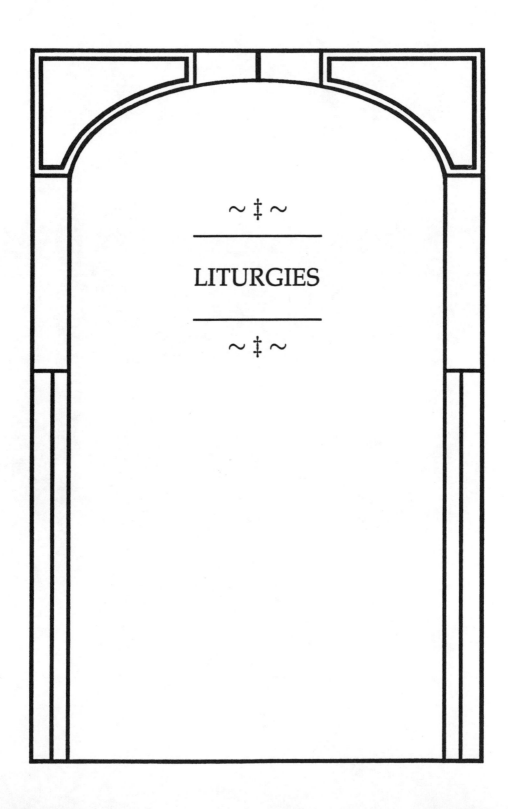

~ ‡ ~

LITURGIES

~ ‡ ~

~ ‡ ~

THE CANON
OF THE EUCHARIST

~ ‡ ~

Celebrant: We thank you, O Holy God, for your Spirit,
which moved over the waters of creation,
to bring beauty and order out of chaos,
to give light in the midst of darkness,
and to bring life in the midst of death.

People: We thank you for the prophets,
who, with eyes of compassion,
proclaimed your presence among your people,
calling them to faithfulness.

Celebrant: We thank you for the disciples in every age,
who, in witness to your love,
have crossed the barriers
of time, place, and taboo,
which separate one people from another.

People: We join our voices with people
of every age and nation,
with angels and archangels,
and with the company of heaven
to proclaim the glory of your name.

All: Holy, Holy, Holy God.
Source of power and love.
The universe is filled with your glory.
Blessings to you from all there is,
and blessed is the one who comes in your name.
Blessing and honor to you forever.
Holy, Holy, Holy God. Amen.

Celebrant: Holy God,
your Spirit transforms our inner creation:
When we are bereft,
feeling there is only failure in our living,

People: you enter our hearts and give us hope.

Celebrant: When we are alone in our despair,

People: you send someone to love and to restore us.

Celebrant: When we weep and cry in sorrow or in pain,

People: you bring us comfort
and the surprise of laughter in our tears.

Celebrant: When we are captive and imprisoned,
by our thoughts and prejudices,
our compulsions and fears,

People: you set us free
enabling us to cross the barriers that divide.

Celebrant: Holy God,
you set us free from all that would bind us
and keep us enslaved.
You bless us by your Spirit
that we might celebrate the future and its hope
in this present hour of need,
and not spend our lives longing
for good times gone by.

People: Holy God,
we thank you for your presence among us
in our past, our present, and our future.

Celebrant: We praise you, O Holy God,
for sending Jesus Christ into this world
to live and die as one of us.
We thank you for the water of his baptism
through which he identified
with all who sin.

People: We thank you for the water of our baptism
through which we are raised
to a new life in Christ,
called to a life of faithfulness and service,
in witness to your love.

Celebrant: We thank you for the fulfillment of expectation
that Christ brought into this world:
for life within our dying,
comfort in the midst of mourning,
and gladness amid our tears.

In a time of darkness, despair, and oppression,
Jesus took bread,
gave thanks to you for it,
broke it,
and gave it to his friends and said,

All: "Take, eat.
This is my body
which is given for you.
Do this in remembrance of me."

Celebrant: After they had eaten,
he took a cup of wine,
gave thanks to you,
and gave it to them saying,

All: "Drink this all of you.
This is my blood of the new Covenant
which is shed for you and for many,
for the forgiveness of sins.
Whenever you drink it,
do this in remembrance of me."

Celebrant: Sanctify this bread and this wine,
O Holy God,
that they may be for us
the body and blood of Christ
which makes us one in Christ
and unites us to you in covenant.
As we eat and drink this bread and wine,
let us hold dear in our hearts those persons
for whom we have prayed.

People: May we continue to lift them
in prayer to you for your healing grace.
Strengthen us also
that we may work and act on their behalf,
and become a source of blessing in their lives.

Celebrant: For it is in remembrance of your call to serve
that we proclaim the mystery of our faith.

All:	Christ has died. Christ is risen. Christ will come again.
Celebrant:	Sanctify us with your Holy Spirit that our hearts may burn with the fire of compassion, laughter, and love. Make us proclaimers of your love and peace in this world full of darkness and despair; for you are the God of our hope and of our salvation.
All:	Blessed are you, O Holy God, who created this world and all that is in it, who has given us light in the darkness since the beginning of time.
Celebrant:	Blessed are you, O Holy God, who nurtures, loves, redeems, and saves your whole creation and all that dwells therein.
All:	We praise your name through Jesus Christ, in the unity of the Holy Spirit all honor and glory be unto you, now and forever. Amen.

~ ‡ ~

A LITURGY FOR THE BLESSING
OF A COUPLE

~ ‡ ~

~ Gathering in God's Name

Dear friends and family, we are gathered here in the presence of God to witness and to bless the covenant and commitment which _____ and _____ make this day with one another. Scripture tells us that we are created in God's image and love and that we are called to be vehicles of love unto one another. Our Savior Jesus Christ said to his disciples, "Love one another, as I have loved you." Fulfilling the two commandments for life that he gave us, to love God and our neighbor, we give praise and glory unto God and enrich the lives of one another. By the love we show unto others shall we be known as followers of Christ. God established a covenant relationship with us founded in love, mercy, forgiveness, and faithfulness. _____ and _____ come here today to commit their lives to a covenant union with one another, to live together faithfully, in love, forgiveness, and mercy. Therefore let us rejoice with them and pledge our love, friendship, and support unto them.

Celebrant: *(addressing the partners each in turn)*
_____ will you promise to live in a covenanted relationship with _____? Will you love *her/him*, comfort *her*, honor and keep *her*, in sickness and in health, and forsaking all others, be faithful to *her* as long as you both shall live?

Partner: I will.

Celebrant:	*(addressing the congregation)*
	Will all you, who witness their vows, do all in your power to support them in their union; will you share their joys, and comfort them in their sorrows?
People:	We will.

~ Proclaiming God's Word

Celebrant:	God's love be with you.
People:	And also with you.
Celebrant:	Let us pray. O gracious and everliving God, you have created us to be the bearers of your love. Look mercifully upon these two persons who come seeking your blessing and assist them with your grace, that with fidelity and lasting love they may honor and keep the vows and promises which they make; through Jesus Christ our Savior we pray. Amen.

One or more passages from Scripture are read. If there is to be a Eucharist, then one reading must be from the Gospels.

> Song of Solomon 2:10–13; 8:6–7a *(Many waters cannot quench love.)*
> 1 Corinthians 13:1–13 *(Love is patient and kind.)*
> Colossians 3:12–17 *(Above all, put on love.)*
> 1 John 4:7–16 *(Love is of God.)*
> Matthew 5:1–10 *(The Beatitudes.)*
> John 15:9–12 *(Love one another as I have loved you.)*

A homily may be preached.

~ The Covenant

One PARTNER faces the other, holding her/his right hand and says:

In the name of God, I _____, take you, _____, to be my beloved, to live together in a covenant of love, mercy, forgiveness, and faithfulness; whether we are rich or poor, in illness or in health, whether life is desirable or wracked with misery and pain, until we are parted by death. This is my solemn vow.

They loose hands, and the second PARTNER takes the first's right hand and says:

In the name of God, I _____, take you, _____, to be my beloved, to live together in a covenant of love, mercy, forgiveness, and faithfulness; whether we are rich or poor, in illness or in health, whether life is desirable or wracked with misery and pain, until we are parted by death. This is my solemn vow.

The CELEBRANT is given the ring/s or other symbol of love to be exchanged and blesses them with these words:

Bless, O God, these rings (or symbol) to be a sign of the covenant by which these persons have bound themselves to one another.

One PARTNER places the ring on the hand of the other and says:

_____, I give you this ring, as a symbol of my promise, and with all that I am and all that I have, I honor you, in the name of God.

This vow is repeated by the other partner if two rings, or symbols, are used.

Celebrant: Now that _____ and _____ have given themselves to each other by solemn vows and the making of a covenant, with the joining of hands and the giving and receiving of rings, I pronounce their love blessed by us and by God's love for us.

~ Praying for the Couple and for the World

Let us pray together in the words our Savior taught us:

> O God in heaven,
> you who are Mother and Father to us all,
> Holy is your name.
> Your reign has come.
> Your will be done
> on earth as in heaven.
> Give us this day
> our daily bread.
> Forgive us our sin
> as we forgive those
> who sin against us.
> Deliver us from evil.
> Save us from the time of trial.
> For all time and all space,
> all power and all glory are yours,
> now and forever. Amen.

*Friends may read one or more of the following prayers or may offer their hopes and
dreams for the couple.*

Eternal God, creator and preserver of all life, author of salvation, and
giver of all grace: Look with favor upon the world you have made, and
especially upon _____ and _____. Amen.

Give them wisdom and devotion in the ordering of their common life,
that each may be to the other a strength in need, a counselor in perplexity,
a comfort in sorrow, and a companion in joy. Amen.

Grant that their wills may be so knit together in your will, and their
spirits in your Spirit, that they may grow in love and peace with you and
one another all the days of their life. Amen.

Give them grace, when they hurt each other, to recognize and acknowledge their fault, and to seek each other's forgiveness and yours.
Amen.

Make their life together a sign of Christ's love to this sinful and broken
world, that unity may overcome estrangement, forgiveness heal guilt,
and joy conquer despair. Amen.

Give them such fulfillment of their mutual affection that they may reach
out in love and concern for others. Amen.

Grant that the bonds of our common humanity, by which all your children are united to one another, and the living to the dead, may be so
transformed by your grace, that your will may be done now and forever;
through Jesus Christ, our Savior. Amen.*

~ The Blessing

The couple kneels.

Most loving God, send your blessing upon these your servants, _____
and _____, that they may so love, honor, and cherish each other in
faithfulness and patience, in wisdom and true godliness, that their home
may be a haven of blessing and peace, through Jesus Christ our Savior,
who lives and reigns with you and the Holy Spirit, one God, forever
and ever. Amen.

---

*The prayers in "Praying for the Couple and for the World" are taken from the marriage
ceremony in the Episcopal *Book of Common Prayer*.

~ Benediction

The blessing of God, whose love created all life and brought you to birth, be with you this day.

The blessing of God, whose love transforms our living and reconciles us to the divine and to one another, be with you always.

The blessing of God, whose love inspires your love, fill you with all spiritual benediction and grace, that you may live faithfully together, and in the age to come, have life everlasting. Amen.

The couple stands.

The Peace

Celebrant: The grace, peace, and love of God be with you.

People: And also with you.

The Eucharist may follow. If not, the couple may embrace and then process out of the room or join their guests.

~ ‡ ~

THE CELEBRATION AND BLESSING OF A JEWISH-CHRISTIAN WEDDING

~ ‡ ~

~ The Gathering

PROCESSIONAL: After all members of the wedding party have taken their places under the hoopa, the ceremony begins.

Rabbi: May you who are here be blessed in the name of the Lord.

If the ceremony takes place in a synagogue, the rabbi adds:

We bless you from the house of the Lord.

Otherwise, the rabbi continues,

May God who is supreme in power, blessing and glory bless this bridegroom and this bride.

The RABBI offers one of the following prayers:

O God, source of holiness, help us to see the sacred dimension of all life. Guide this bridegroom and bride to the realization of sanctity and devotion every day as today. Help them to renew their love continually, as you renew creation. May their concern for each other reflect your concern for all; may their loving faithfulness reflect your love. Throughout the years may they hallow life together, that the home they establish become a blessing. May your light illumine their lives. And let us say: Amen.

This service was composed by Rabbi Harold White, chaplain at Georgetown University, Washington, D.C., and the author. The Christian portion of the ceremony is taken from the Episcopal *Book of Common Prayer*. Rabbi White is the source for the Jewish portion.

or

In happiness and joy we thank God for the divine blessing of love that we celebrate today, formally consecrating the love of _____ and _____ for each other. May they always rejoice in their love, graced by delight through their mutual affection. O Lord, our God, source of all blessing, fulfill every worthy wish of their hearts. Open their eyes to the beauty and mystery of the love they hold for each other, every day as today. May their life together embrace and nurture the promise of this moment, so that all who know them will call them truly blessed. And let us say: Amen.

The PRIEST says the following:

Dearly beloved: We have come together in the presence of God to witness and bless the joining together of this man and this woman in Holy Matrimony. The bond and covenant of marriage was established by God in creation, and Holy Scripture commends it to be honored among all people.

The union of husband and wife in heart, body and mind is intended by God for their mutual joy; for the help and comfort given one another in prosperity and adversity; and, when it is God's will, for the procreation of children and their nurture in the knowledge and love of God. Therefore marriage is not to be entered into unadvisedly or lightly, but reverently, deliberately, and in accordance with the purposes for which it was instituted by God.

Into this holy union

_____ [*full name*] _____ and _____ [*full name*]_____ now come to be joined.

If any of you can show just cause why they may not lawfully be married, speak now; or else forever hold your peace.

The PRIEST says to the persons to be married:

I require and charge you both, here in the presence of God, that if either of you know any reason why you may not be united in marriage lawfully and in accordance with God's Word, you do now confess it.

~ The Declaration of Consent

Priest:	*(to the woman)*
	_____, will you have this man to be your husband, to live together in the covenant of marriage? Will you love him, comfort him, honor and keep him, in sickness and in health, and, forsaking all others, be faithful to him as long as you both shall live?
Woman:	I will.
Priest:	*(to the man)*
	_____, will you have this woman to be your wife, to live together in the covenant of marriage? Will you love her, comfort her, honor and keep her, in sickness and in health, and, forsaking all others, be faithful to her as long as you both shall live?
Man:	I will.

~ The Blessing of Family and Friends

Priest:	*(addresses the congregation)*
	It is important to know that in our times of joy and in times of sorrow, our families and friends will be with us to support us and to share our lives. Therefore, I ask you to make a commitment to the bride and groom at this time. Will all you witnessing these promises do all in your power to uphold _____ and _____ in their marriage?
People:	We will.
Priest:	Who from the bride's family blesses this marriage?
Those speaking for the bride's family answer:	
	I do.
Priest:	Who from the groom's family blesses this marriage?
Those speaking for the groom's family answer:	
	I do.

Priest: Let us pray.

O gracious and everliving God, you have created us male and female in your image: Look mercifully upon _____ and _____ who come to you seeking your blessing and assist them with your grace, that with true fidelity and steadfast love they may honor and keep the promises and vows they make. Through their love may your name be praised. Amen.

~ The Proclamation of the Word of God

Genesis 1:26–28, 31a *(God created humankind in the divine image.)*
Song of Solomon 2:10–13, 8:6–7 *(My beloved speaks.)*
Colossians 3:12–17 *(Love binds everything together in harmony.)*
1 Corinthians 13:1–13 *(Love is patient and kind.)*

The RABBI reads from Baal Shem Tov:

From every human being there rises a light that reaches straight to heaven. And when two souls that are destined for each other find one another, their streams of light flow together and a single brighter light goes forth from their united being.

The couple may light a single candle from two candles.

~ The Marriage

The PRIEST instructs the MAN to face the woman, take her right hand in his, and repeat after the priest, saying:

In the name of God, I, _____, take you, _____, to be my wife, to have and to hold from this day forward, for better for worse, for richer for poorer, in sickness and in health, to love and to cherish, until we are parted by death. This is my solemn vow.

They loose their hands. The WOMAN, facing the man, takes his right hand in hers and, repeating after the priest, says:

In the name of God, I, _____, take you, _____, to be my husband, to have and to hold from this day forward, for better for worse, for richer for poorer, in sickness and in health, to love and to cherish, until we are parted by death. This is my solemn vow.

They loose their hands.

The rings are given to the RABBI, who may say a blessing upon them. The rabbi instructs the MAN to place the ring on the forefinger of the woman and to say:

By this ring you are consecrated to me as my wife in accordance with the law of Moses and the people of Israel.

The RABBI instructs the WOMAN to respond:

In accepting this ring, I pledge you all my love and devotion.

The RABBI instructs the WOMAN to place the ring on the forefinger of the man and to say:

By this ring you are consecrated to me as my husband in accordance with the law of Moses and the people of Israel.

The RABBI instructs the MAN to respond:

In accepting this ring, I pledge you all my love and devotion.

~ The Tying of the Knot

The PRIEST asks the couple to join right hands and explains to the congregation the meaning of wrapping the stole around the hands, signifying the tying of the knot, a phrase used to mean "getting married." The priest then says,

Now that _____ and _____ have given themselves to each other by solemn vows, with the joining of hands and the giving and receiving of ring/s, I pronounce they are husband and wife, in the name of God. Those whom God has joined together let no one put asunder.

People: Amen.

~ The Drinking of Wine

A cup of wine is shared by the bride and groom. The rabbi or a cantor recites in Hebrew while the couple drinks.

~ The Prayers

The priest or a member of the family or one or more friends lead the prayers:

Eternal God, creator and preserver of all life, author of salvation, and giver of all grace: Look with favor upon the world you have made, and especially upon _____ and _____, whom you make one flesh in Holy Matrimony. Amen.

Give them wisdom and devotion in the ordering of their common life, that each may be to the other a strength in need, a counselor in perplexity, a comfort in sorrow, and a companion in joy. Amen.

Grant that their wills may be so knit together in your will, and their spirits in your Spirit that they may grow in love and peace with you and one another all the days of their life. Amen.

Give them grace when they hurt each other to recognize and acknowledge their fault and to seek each other's forgiveness and yours. Amen.

Make their life together a sign of your love to this sinful and broken world, that unity may overcome estrangement, forgiveness heal guilt, and joy conquer despair. Amen.

Bestow on them, if it is your will, the gift and heritage of children and the grace to bring them up to know you, to love you, and to serve you. Amen.

Give them such fulfillment of their mutual affection that they may reach out in love and concern for others. Amen.

Grant that all married persons who have witnessed these vows may find their lives strengthened and their loyalties confirmed. Amen.

Grant that the bonds of our common humanity, by which all your children are united to one another and the living to the dead, may be so transformed by your grace that your will may be done on earth as it is in heaven, to the glory of your name, now and forever. Amen.

~ The Six Blessings

The rabbi or a member of the family reads the blessings:

1. You abound in blessings, Lord our God, source of all creation, creator of the fruit of the vine, symbol of human joy.

2. You abound in blessings, Lord our God, source of all creation, all of whose creations reflect your glory.

3. You abound in blessings, Lord our God, source of all creation, creator of human beings.

4. You abound in blessings, Lord our God, source of all creation, who created man and woman in your image that they might live, love, and so perpetuate life. You abound in blessings, Lord, creator of human beings.

5. We all rejoice as these two persons, overcoming separateness, unite in joy. You abound in blessings, Lord, permitting us to share in others' joy.

6. May these lovers rejoice as did the first man and woman in the primordial Garden of Eden. You abound in blessings, Lord our God, source of joy for bride and groom.

~ The Blessing of the Marriage

The RABBI and PRIEST say the blessing from the Book of Deuteronomy, alternating in Hebrew and English.

May God bless you and guard you.
May God show you favour and be gracious to you.
May God show you kindness and grant you peace. Amen.

~ The Breaking of the Glass

The RABBI explains the symbolism of the breaking of the glass. A glass is placed on the floor near the man's foot; the man breaks it by stomping on it.

People: Mazeltov!

Priest: The peace and love of God be always with you.

People: And also with you.

The couple greet one another with a kiss and then process down the aisle.

~ ‡ ~

LITURGY FOR DIVORCE

~ ‡ ~

~ The Gathering of the People

Dearly beloved: We have come together in the presence of God to witness and bless the separation of this man and this woman who have been bonded in the covenant of marriage. The courts have acknowledged their divorce and we, this day, gather to support them as they give their blessing to one another as each seeks a new life.

In creation, God made the cycle of life to be birth, life, and death; and God has given us the hope of new life through the Resurrection of Jesus Christ, our Savior. The Church recognizes that relationships follow this pattern. While the couple have promised in good faith to love until parted by death, in some marriages the love between a wife and a husband comes to an end sooner. Love dies, and when that happens we recognize that the bonds of marriage, based on love, also may be ended.

God calls us to right relationships based on love, compassion, mutuality, and justice. Whenever any of these elements is absent from a marital relationship, then that partnership no longer reflects the intentionality of God.

The Good News of the Gospel of Jesus Christ is that we are forgiven our sins and our failures, we are raised from the dead and restored to a new life. The death of love, like the death of the grave, has no power to rob us of the life that is intended for the people of God.

Thus we gather this day to support and bless _____ and _____ as they confess their brokenness, forgive one another for their transgressions, receive God's blessing, celebrate the new growth that has occurred in each of them, and make commitments for a new life.

~ The Declaration of Consent

Celebrant:	*(to the man)*
	_____, do you enter into this parting of your own free will; do you confess before God, _____, and the Church that you repent your brokenness that kept you in a destructive relationship? Do you seek forgiveness for the mutual respect and justice that you have failed to give and set your spouse free of this relationship, that you and she may receive from God and from one another the gift of new life and move toward health and wholeness once again?
Man:	I do.
Celebrant:	*(to the woman)*
	_____ do you enter into this parting of your own free will; do you confess before God, _____, and the Church that you repent your brokenness that kept you in a destructive relationship? Do you seek forgiveness for the mutual respect and justice that you have failed to give and set your spouse free of this relationship, that you and he may receive from God and from one another the gift of new life and move toward health and wholeness once again?
Woman:	I do.

~ The Ministry of the Word

Celebrant:	The Lord be with you.
People:	And also with you.
Celebrant:	Let us pray.
	O gracious and ever-living God, you have created us male and female in your image: Look mercifully upon _____ and _____, who come to you seeking your blessing. Forgive them for forsaking their vows, and for the pain that they have caused one another. Restore each of them by your grace to a new life of hope, renewal, and growth, and keep them ever in the love of your mercy, through Jesus Christ our Savior. Amen.

A Reading from Scripture

> Luke 15:1–7 *(Repentance and forgiveness.)*
> Luke 9:42b–48 *(Your faith has made you well.)*
> Psalm 55:12–23 *(Women who feel rejected.)*

> *The choice of a reading depends upon the individuals' need,*
> *whether for forgiveness or wholeness, or both.*

～ The Undoing of the Vows

The MAN faces the woman, takes her right hand, and says:

In the name of God, I, _____, release you, _____, from your vow to be my wife. I thank you for the love and support you have given me. I ask your forgiveness for my part in the failure of our marriage.

The WOMAN faces the man, takes his right hand, and says:

In the name of God, I, _____, release you, _____, from your vow to be my husband. I thank you for the love and support you have given me. I ask your forgiveness for my part in the failure of our marriage.

The CELEBRANT asks each in turn to return their rings:

_____, I give you this ring, which you gave me as a symbol of our marriage. In returning it, I set you free. I pray you will find peace and joy in your new life.

The rings are given to the celebrant, who places them upon the altar, or the man and woman may place the rings there themselves.

The CELEBRANT says:

I place these rings upon the altar to symbolize that your lives are lived in the mercy and love of God.

Or, if the couple choose to place their own rings on the altar, the CELEBRANT may say:

These rings are placed upon the altar to symbolize that your lives are lived in the mercy and love of God.

~ The Prayers

The Lord's Prayer

O God in heaven,
You who are Mother and Father
to us all,
Holy is your name.
Your reign has come.
Your will be done,
on earth as it is in heaven.
Give us today our daily bread.
Forgive us our sin
as we forgive those
who sin against us.
Deliver us from evil.
Save us from the time of trial.
For all time and all space,
all power and all glory are yours;
now and forever. Amen.

Let us pray.

Eternal God, creator and preserver of all life, author of salvation and giver of grace: Look with favor upon the world you have made and for which your Son gave his life, and especially upon _____ and _____, who come to you seeking your blessing. Grant unto them grace in moving from the old ways and wisdom in the ordering of their new lives. Amen.

Grant that each may know the power of your love to transform death into life and to bring forth the discovery of new identity out of pain. Teach them to trust once again and restore their hope, that once more they may view the world through love-filled eyes. Amen.

Bestow on them your Spirit, that _____ and _____ may be guided and sustained by you in the choices they individually make. Inspire the service they offer to the world that it may be distinguished by compassion for all. By your grace, may each become a witness to your forgiving and healing love as they reach out to care for the needs of others. Amen.

Make their individual lives a sign of Christ's love to this sinful and broken world, that forgiveness may heal guilt, joy conquer despair, and trust be forever placed in you. Amen.

The man and woman kneel.

Most gracious God, we give you thanks for your tender love in sending Jesus Christ to come among us, to be born of a human mother, and to make the way of the cross to be the way of life. Defend _____ and _____ from every enemy. Lead them both into all peace, to a renewal of life, and the hope of wholeness and love. Bless them in their separate lives, in their work, in their rest, and in their play, in their joys and in their sorrows, in their life and in their death. Finally, in your mercy, bring each to that table where your saints feast forever in the blessing of your presence and love, through Jesus Christ, who with you and the Holy Spirit, lives and reigns, One God, for ever and ever. Amen.*

Benediction

The blessing of God whose breath gives life
be with you always.

The blessing of God whose
love is forgiving
set you free from guilt and despair.

The blessing of God
who sanctifies your living
be with you this day,
to lead you to a new life
of hope, peace, love, and service.

May God be praised and glorified through your lives,
now and forever. Amen.

---

*The preceding prayer contains, by design, some familiar words from the wedding service of the Episcopal Church. They are to be found in "The Celebration and Blessing of a Marriage," *The Book of Common Prayer*, © Church Pension Fund.

~ ‡ ~

THE CELEBRATION AND BLESSING
OF A SECOND MARRIAGE

~ ‡ ~

~ Gathering in God's Name

The CELEBRANT welcomes all with these words:

Dear family and friends, we gather with joy to celebrate and to bless the marriage of _____ and _____ as they come together seeking God's blessing upon their love and their creation of a new life. The bond and covenant of marriage was established by God in creation and it is intended for their mutual joy and fulfillment. _____ and _____ have not entered into this covenant lightly. They are aware of the responsibility, commitment, perseverance, patience, honesty, trust, and faithfulness that love demands. Each has experienced the death of a relationship and knows the pain and sorrow of failure. Each understands the joy of forgiveness and the renewal experienced in life when one has another chance to love and to be loved.

The Church teaches us that such opportunities are an experience of the resurrection through Jesus Christ that God intends for us all. In the midst of endings we shall encounter new beginnings; out of our sorrows we shall know joy; where we thought there was only death, we shall receive life. Such a blessing has been bestowed on _____ and _____ in the love they have found in one another. Therefore let us rejoice with them and be glad.

If any of you can show just cause why they may not be married lawfully, and in accordance with God's word, speak now, or else forever hold your peace.

The CELEBRANT addresses the bride and groom:

I require and charge you both, that if either of you know why you should not be married lawfully or in accordance with God's word, you do now confess it.

The CELEBRANT addresses the family of the bride (i.e., the children; if there are none, then her parents or living relatives):

Who from the bride's family blesses this marriage?

The CHILDREN or other family members answer in words of their own choosing or simply say:

I do.

The CELEBRANT addresses the family of the groom (i.e., the children; if there are none, then her parents or living relatives):

Who from the groom's family blesses this marriage?

The CHILDREN or other family members answer in words of their own choosing or simply say:

I do.

The CELEBRANT addresses the congregation:

Will all you who witness these promises do all in your power to support _____ and _____ in their marriage?

The congregation responds:

We will.

CELEBRANT:

Let us pray.

Most loving God, we thank you for the grace bestowed upon _____ and _____ in their love for one another. Grant unto them the abundance of your blessing and love that they may live faithfully together, grow in wisdom and respect for one another, and be a sign of hope and renewal in this broken world; in the name of Jesus Christ we pray. Amen.

~ Hearing the Word of God

Deuteronomy 30:9–14 *(The word is very near you...in your heart.)*
Psalm 19
Revelation 21:1–5 *(Behold, I make all things new; an inclusive-language text is necessary for this reading.)*
Mark 16:1–7 *(He has risen; he is not here.)*

A hymn may be sung between the Epistle and Gospel, and also after the Gospel reading.

A homily may be preached.

~ The Marriage

The MAN faces the woman, takes her right hand in his, and says:

In the name of God, I, _____, take you, _____, to be my wife from this day forward, to be faithful to you in good times and in bad, whether rich or poor, whether sick or in health, to love and to cherish, until we are parted by death. This is my solemn vow.

The WOMAN faces the man, takes his right hand in hers, and says:

In the name of God, I, _____, take you, _____, to be my husband from this day forward, to be faithful to you in good times and in bad, whether rich or poor, whether sick or in health, to love and to cherish, until we are parted by death. This is my solemn vow.

They loosen their hands. The CELEBRANT is given the ring/s and says:

Bless, O God, these rings to be a sign of the vows by which _____ and _____ have bound themselves to each other, through Jesus Christ we pray. Amen.

The COUPLE in turn give one another the rings and say:

_____, I give you this ring as a symbol of my vow, and with all that I am, I honor you, in the name of God.

The COUPLE joins right hands. The CELEBRANT ties the stole around their hands and says:

Now that _____ and _____ have given themselves to each other by solemn vows, joining hands, and the giving and receiving of rings, I pronounce they are husband and wife in the name of God. Those whom God has joined together let no one part.

People: Amen.

~ The Prayers

Celebrant: Let us pray together in the words our Savior Christ has taught us:

The Lord's Prayer

*Prayers from the marriage service in the Episcopal **Book of Common Prayer** may be used.*

~ The Blessing of the Marriage

Most loving God, you made manifest to the world the depth of your love through Jesus Christ, who, through his resurrection, revealed to us the power of your love to give us life. Send your blessing upon _____ and _____ that they faithfully may keep the vows which they have made this day. May the love, honor, and respect which they have given to each other be the basis of the manner in which they respond to others, that their lives may be a sign in this world of your love and their home a blessing to all, through Jesus Christ, who lives and reigns with you and the Holy Spirit, now and forever. Amen.

The husband and wife kneel.

Celebrant: The blessing of God,
who made you male and female,
be with you as you become one flesh.

The blessing of God,
whose love transforms all things,
be with you in this new beginning.

The blessing of God,
whose Spirit inspires all love,
be with you as you fulfill your vows,
now and forever. Amen.

The couple rise and greet one another with a kiss.

Celebrant: The peace and love of God be always with you.

People: And also with you.

The service may end here or continue with the Eucharist.

~ ‡ ~

BLESSING OF THE HOME

~ ‡ ~

~ The Gathering

The people gather in the home to be blessed. If there is to be a Eucharist, one of the participants might bake the bread.

The homeowner/s greet their guests in a manner appropriate to them and explain what the evening means to them.

~ The Proclaiming of God's Word

Celebrant: Let us pray.

Bless, most loving God,
this home and all who dwell herein.
May it be for *her/him/them*
a sanctuary of rest and peace,
of re-creation and love.
May it be a place of hospitality
for friends and strangers alike.
May all who enter here
know the presence of your love;
in Christ's name we pray.
Amen.

Friends or family members read the lessons. If the Eucharist is to be celebrated, one reading must be from the Gospels. Possible selections:

Genesis 18:1–8 *(Abraham and Sarah show hospitality to strangers.)*
1 Peter 1:23–2:5 *(Like living stones be built into a spiritual house.)*
Matthew 6:25–33 *(Do not be anxious about your life.)*

A homily may be given.

~ The Blessing of the Rooms

The CELEBRANT takes the bowl of salt and the bowl of water and combines them, saying:

Salt is a symbol of purification,
and water is a symbol of new life in Christ.
Bless these elements of your creation, O God,
that as we sprinkle them in each room
all fears of darkness and evil may be banished
and the life celebrated in each room
bring glory to your name.   Amen.

The family and friends move from room to room with special prayers said in each room. A member of the household, or a friend, may carry:

a lighted candle: symbol of the light of Christ
a Bible: symbol of God's word
a bell: symbol of casting out evil spirits
a bowl of water: symbol of purification

In each room, a prayer is offered, water is sprinkled, the candle and Bible are raised, and the bell is rung.

The Entrance

Keep watch, O loving God, over their going out and their coming in. Let the stranger be welcomed and refreshed, let the friend find gracious hospitality in your name. Send the members of this home forth strengthened to do your will, and bring them safely home again to find peace in your presence here where they dwell; in Christ's name we pray.   Amen.

The Dining Room

Blessed are you, O God, ruler of the universe. You give us food and drink to sustain our lives and to offer hospitality to others. May this room be a gathering place where the family's life is nurtured and where friendships are strengthened as bodies are nourished and fed; in Christ's name we pray. Amen.

The Kitchen

We thank you, O God, for those who lovingly prepare food for us to eat, and for those who clean up the messes that we make. May this kitchen be a place of remembrance that all that we have is a gift of your bounty; in Christ's name we pray. Amen.

The Den or Study

O God of wisdom and truth, grant that this room may be a place of learning and reflection, that those who dwell herein may grow in knowledge and love of you and in compassion for their neighbor; in Christ's name we pray. Amen.

The Family Room

O God, you created us to laugh and to play. Grant that in this room all may find the joy of shared laughter and delight that they may know the blessings and re-creation of love; in Christ's name we pray. Amen.

The Master Bedroom

Bless the occupant of this room, O God, and grant to *her/him/them* rest from a busy day, the re-creation that sleep and dreams do bring, and the full companionship that sex and love provide; in the name of Christ we pray. Amen.

A Child's Bedroom

Bless the child who lives in this room; grant *her/him* protection in the night, refreshment in the morning, that *she* may delight in the wonder and mystery of all you have created; in Christ's name we pray. Amen.

The Guest Room

Grant to all guests who sleep here the blessing of kindliness and gracious hospitality. May they take with them the joy of these blessings to share with others who are alone and to offer to those who need their love; in Christ's name we pray. Amen.

A Bathroom

You have blessed us, O God, with the gift of water. It cleanses our bodies, restores us within, offers us opportunities to play, and reminds us of your gift to us of eternal life. Bless this room which is set aside for the care of our bodies and grant health and wholeness to all who come herein; in Christ's name we pray. Amen.

The Workshop

You have given us talents to use, O God of creation. Bless those who work with their hands to create objects of usefulness and beauty. May they remind us all to claim the gifts you have given us; in Christ's name we pray. Amen.

The Laundry Room

Bless this room and the labor of all who perform acts of service for the members of this family. May they be an example to us all of the service you call us to do for others; in Christ's name we pray. Amen.

The Garage

Jesus was born in a stable, not unlike the garage of our household. May this room that stores the essential tools of our lives be a reminder to us to care for those who are homeless and those who lack the tools and skills for employment; in the name of Christ we pray. Amen.

The Living Room

Bless this room, O God, where family, friends, and strangers gather. May it be a place of hospitality where friendships are enriched, joys and sorrows shared, and laughter and love prevail. Bless all who enter here that they may find their minds, bodies, and souls refreshed in the companionship of this home; in the name of Jesus Christ we pray. Amen.

~ The Peace

Celebrant: The peace of God be with you always.

People: And also with you.

The people greet one another with hugs.

~ The Eucharist

If the Eucharist is to be celebrated, the bread and wine are placed on the table. This may be done in the living room with all seated around a coffee table, or in the dining room with all standing around the table there.

~ Post-Communion Prayer

We thank you, O God, for feeding us with spiritual food of the Body and Blood of Jesus Christ. We thank you for giving us homes where we may shelter our families (or extended families) and offer hospitality to our friends. Therefore we praise you, joining our voices with angels and archangels to proclaim the glory of your name:

All: Holy, Holy, Holy God.
Source of power and love.
The universe is filled with your glory.
Blessing to you from all there is,
and blessed is the one who comes in your name.
Blessing and honor to you forever.
Holy, Holy, Holy God. Amen.

~ Benediction

Celebrant: The blessing of God,
the creator of life,
be with you this day.

The blessing of God,
whose love claims us as God's own,
be with you always.

The blessing of God,
who inspires our love,
open your hearts
to those who have no home or family. Amen.

~ ‡ ~

LITURGY FOR SAYING GOOD-BYE
TO A FORMER HOME

~ ‡ ~

~ The Gathering of the People

Friends and family gather in the home. Refreshments may be served.

A song may be sung.

When everyone is gathered, a member of the household says:

Leader: Blessed be God who has nurtured us in this home.

People: Blessings be upon all who have lived here
for the hospitality and love they have shown.

Leader: Let us pray.

Loving God, we thank you for the life we have known in
this home, for the riches of our memories, for the laughter
and tears we have shared, for the love that has bound us
together. Grant that our memories may guide us in the
choices that lie ahead, our laughter and tears may keep
us open to the needs of others, and our love may keep us
close though we are far apart; in the name of Christ we
pray. Amen.

~ Proclaiming the Word of God

One or more selections from Scripture are read. If there is to be a Eucharist, one must be a Gospel:

> Genesis 12:1–4 *(Abraham leaves home.)*
> Jeremiah 31:31–34 *(A new Covenant.)*
> Mark 14:3–9 *(Jesus revealed as the Messiah in a home.)*
> Mark 10:17–22 *(A young man with many possessions.)*
> Mark 9:33–37 *(The greatest must be like a child.)*

~ The Blessing of the Rooms

The procession from room to room begins.

All are invited to share their memories in each of the rooms. A symbol may be left in each room for the new owners to discover. If the walls are to be repainted, someone may wish to write a memory on them in pencil, or to hide a message in the closet.

At the end of the sharing of memories in each room, the person responsible for that room offers thanks for all that has been shared and names a hope for the new occupant.

The procession moves on to the next room. When all the rooms have been visited, the gathering returns to the primary room of choice, e.g., living room, dining room.

~ Making Eucharist or Agape

The Eucharist may be celebrated.

If there is no Eucharist, the service closes with a member of the family feeding each guest a piece of bread. This symbolizes the nurturing and love that they have shared as they have fed one another over the years of their friendship.

~ The Blessing

Leader: Let us pray.

We thank you, O God, for the gift of friendships and for the love that we have known in this dwelling place. We have been a blessing to one another over these years. We ask you to give your blessing to all of us gathered here this day. May our love for one another continue to grow and to spread beyond ourselves to all who are in need of love, compassion, and care; in the name of Christ, we pray. Amen.

~ Benediction

The blessing of God,
who created us to live in community,
be with you, whether near or far.

The blessing of God,
whose love is with us wherever we go,
keep you close in one another's hearts.

The blessing of God,
whose Spirit sanctifies your living,
be with you always,
and make your new home a haven of blessing for all.

Amen.

~ The Closing

A song may be sung.
Gifts may be shared (see note below).
A meal may be served.
A reception/open house may be held.

The celebration continues in whatever form is appropriate to the household.

NOTE

It is appropriate to plant something in the garden as a gift for the new owner and as a symbol of all that is left behind. The planting could take place during the journey through the spaces of the home, the garden being one of the places visited. Or it may take place at the end, as the summation of the whole event. If the weather doesn't permit this, perhaps some gift could be left in the house that is symbolic of the family's or individual's life. This could be done at the end of the ceremony.

The family or individual might wish to give each guest some token from the house as a symbol of the life that has been shared in this place of friendship and love.

The guests might be invited to bring a poem, an old photo, or memento, or they may wish to bring a gift for the new home. The exchanging of memories is a gift in itself so other gifts aren't necessary, but those who wish to bring a gift should do so.

If there is a feast, each guest might bring a favorite dish that is a reminder of dinners shared in the past and yet to come.

~ ‡ ~

A RITUAL FOR
REBUILDING MEMORIES
AFTER A FIRE

~ ‡ ~

~ Gathering of the People

A welcome is given by the person or persons whose home has burnt.

Prayer:

Bless, O God, _____, that their lives as well as their home may be restored to fullness and peace. May this experience of devastation make our hearts kinder toward those in need. May the destruction of this home open our hearts to those who are homeless. May our lives be filled with love for you and our neighbor and not for things that are consumed; in the name of Jesus Christ we pray. Amen.

~ Proclaiming God's Word

Genesis 12:1–9 *(Abraham leaving home.)*
Psalm 40 *(I waited patiently for the Lord.)*
Revelation 21:1–5 *(Behold I make all things new.)*
Matthew 6:19–33 *(Do not lay up treasures on earth.)*
Matthew 7:24–19 *(Build a house upon a rock.)*

~ Sharing Memories and Love

Out of this sharing, a book of memories may be created to build some continuity with what has been lost.

Stories and memories are recounted.

These may be written down beforehand so they may be added to the book afterward or they might be taped.

Photos from different periods of the individual's or family's history can be brought as gifts and memories shared. These can be added to the book.

~ Praying for All

Leader: Let us pray in the words our Savior taught us.

The Lord's Prayer is said.

Leader: God's peace to all who are gathered here.

People: In your love, O God, hear our prayer.

Leader: God's blessing be upon all who are homeless.

People: In your love, O God, hear our prayer.

Leader: God's blessing be upon all who are hungry.

People: In your love, O God, hear our prayer.

Leader: God's blessing be upon all who are sick.

People: In your love, O God, hear our prayer.

Leader: God's blessing be upon all who are dying.

People: In your love, O God, hear our prayer.

Leader: I invite your prayers for this family.

The people may offer their own prayers for the family, their loss, and the hope of a new life.

Leader: Hear the prayers of your people, O God, and grant your blessings unto all who call upon your love this day; in the name of Jesus Christ we pray. Amen.

～ The Peace

The hostess or host of the evening says:
> The peace and love of God be with you.

People: And also with you.

The Peace and hugs are shared. The service may conclude at this point and a meal be shared. Or it may continue with the Eucharist, which may also be followed by a meal or light refreshment.

～ Making Eucharist

Bread and wine are brought to the table around which the people gather. The youngest members of the family whose house was burnt might be chosen to bring these elements.

*As this is an informal gathering, the Eucharist might be celebrated according to one of the forms on pages 402–5 in the Episcopal **Book of Common Prayer**; or the following may be used.*

Celebrant: Blessed are you, O God of creation. We give thanks to you for the splendors of the universe and for all creatures that you have made.

People: Blessed are you, O God of love.

Celebrant: Blessed are you, O God, for the revelation of yourself throughout history. We thank you especially this day for Abraham and Sarah who trusted in you to guide them and to lead them to a new home. We thank you for all the prophets, martyrs, apostles, and faithful followers of Christ who have taught us to wait patiently and to trust in your providence. We thank you for all who have made known to us the sure foundation of your love.

People: Blessed are you, O God of love.

Celebrant: Blessed are you, O God, for this gathering of friendship and love. You have knit us together as one extended family to share our joys and our sorrows. We ask your blessing upon this family in this time of destruction and loss. We thank you for the richness of the life we have shared, for our common memories, and for the hope of days to come.

People: Blessed are you, O God of love.

Celebrant: Blessed are you, O God, for sending your Chosen One, Jesus Christ, to be the Savior of the world. We thank you for the example of love he has given us. We thank you for the ministry of service to which he has called us. But most especially do we thank you this day for the gift of remembrance given unto us.

The celebrant lifts the bread and all lay hands upon it.

Celebrant: On the night in which he was handed over to suffering and death, he took bread, and when he had given thanks to you, he broke it and said,

All: "Take, eat. This is my Body which is given for you. Do this in remembrance of me."

The celebrant lifts the wine and all lay hands upon it.

Celebrant: After supper, he took the cup of wine, gave thanks, and said,

All: "Drink this all of you. This is my Blood of the new Covenant which is shed for you and for many for the forgiveness of sins. Whenever you drink it, do this in remembrance of me."

Celebrant: Therefore we proclaim the mystery of faith.

All: Blessed are you, O God of love.
We remember Jesus' death.
We proclaim the resurrection of Jesus Christ.
We await the coming of Christ again.

Celebrant: Sanctify, O God of love, these gifts of bread and wine by your Holy Spirit, that they may be for us the Body and Blood of Jesus Christ, the holy food and drink of unending life for us, which fill us with your blessing.

People: Blessed are you, O God of love.

Celebrant: Sanctify us also by your Holy Spirit that we may proclaim with power and hope your blessing and glory, and show forth our thanks in compassion and love for our neighbors. We thank you for the promise of making all things new and ask your blessing especially this *day/night* upon _____ as *she/he/they* begin life again. Receive our prayers through Jesus Christ. By Christ, and with Christ, and in Christ, all honor and glory be to you O God of love, now and forever.

People: Blessed are you, O God of love, forever and ever. Amen.

The bread is broken in silence.

The bread and wine are passed from one to another around the circle. When all have been fed, the celebrant continues.

Celebrant: We thank you, O God of love, for feeding us with these holy mysteries, the Body and Blood of Jesus Christ. Therefore we praise you, joining our voices with those of heaven to proclaim your glory.

The Sanctus is said or sung as the post-communion prayer.

Celebrant: The blessing of God,
whose love gave you life,
be with you today.

People: Blessed are you, O God of love.

Celebrant: The blessing of God, whose love makes all things new, be with you as you rebuild your lives.

People: Blessed are you, O God of love.

Celebrant: The blessing of God,
whose love empowers us to love,
be with you as you serve in Christ's name.

People: Blessed are you, O God of love now and forever. Amen.

~ Enjoying a Feast

The people enjoy refreshments or a meal with one another. Each friend might bring a favorite dish that has been shared in the past to evoke memories of times shared.

~ ‡ ~

RITUALS CONCERNING ABORTION

~ ‡ ~

LITURGY AT THE TIME OF CHOOSING WHETHER OR NOT TO HAVE AN ABORTION

~ Gathering in God's Name

The woman, family, and friends gather in God's name. This is a very intimate service. It may take place in a home or a chapel in a church. If there is not a sensitive priest known to the woman facing the abortion, then a friend or mother may take the role of the leader.

Leader: Blessed are you,
loving God, Mother of all.

People: Holy is your name,
now and forever.

Leader: Eternal Womb
from whence all came,

People: We lift our hearts to you.
Heal our wounds.

Leader: Mother of the world,
bless us.

People: Hear our cries
and grant us peace.

Leader: Let us pray.
Loving God, all hearts are open to you, all desires known, and from you, no secrets are hid. Cleanse the thoughts of our hearts that we may love you, and praise your holy name with our acts this day and forever more. Amen

~ The Word of God Proclaimed

One of the following readings from Scripture is read as well as any passage that is particularly meaningful to the woman.

Revelation 21:1–5 *(Behold, I make all things new.)*
Mark 14:1–9 *(She has done what she could.)*
John 1:1–5 *(In the beginning was the Word; an inclusive-language text is essential.)*

Response to God's Word

If the woman has chosen to have an abortion, a letter to the dead child written by the mother may be read by her or by some one of her choosing. The letter may express her feelings, her thoughts about the abortion, what she would have liked to say to the child.

If the woman has chosen not to have an abortion and to keep her child, a letter expressing her hopes and dreams for her child may be read.

~ Prayers for One Another

Leader: Mother of all,
we ask your blessing upon _____.

People: Hear our prayer, O God our Mother.

Leader: Bless all who face the choice of abortion. Grant them wisdom to make their choice, courage to act upon it, and the knowledge of your love.

People: Hear our prayer, O God our Mother.

Leader: Grant unto all women the support and love that we offer unto _____ this day and always. Bind us close in your love and keep us faithful in our friendships.

People: Hear our prayer, O God our Mother.

Leader: Let us ask God's mercy and forgiveness upon all our lives.

Confession

Hear our prayer, O God our Mother. Forgive us our sins as we forgive those who have sinned against us. Forgive us our passivity, our doubts, our guilt, and our shame. Empower us to forgive ourselves that we may receive the fullness of your forgiveness and grace; in Jesus Christ's name we pray. Amen.

Absolution

Loving God, you have given power to your priests to pronounce absolution; give to this your daughter _____, your love to absolve her guilt, remove her fear, heal her wounds, and make whole her body, that she may live her life reconciled to you and to her child, with the opportunity to begin a new life sustained by your Holy Spirit, now and forever. Amen.

~ Act of Dedication

The mother makes a dedication in the name of the child and asks for the community's support to keep her vow. The promise should be personal, specific, and attainable.

Example: *"In the name of my child, I promise I will give $ _____ every month for the coming year to support a homeless child...."*

               "In the name of my child, I promise I will plant a garden on the street where all who pass by may see the abundance of God's grace."

~ The Laying On of Hands

People: We lay our hands upon you in the name of our Savior, Jesus Christ, beseeching God to uphold you and to fill you with grace, that you may know the healing power of God's divine love. We give you our love, promising to stand by you through this decision and in the days to come. Amen.

～ The Peace

Leader: The peace and love of God be with you this day.

People: And also with you.

The people exchange the Peace with hugs. It make take as long as necessary.

If the woman has chosen to have an abortion, it is suggested that the letter that she has written be burned and the ashes buried in a suitable place. This helps to give a tangible sense of letting go and of burial.

The service may conclude here or the people may make Eucharist. It is appropriate to use homemade bread. If the Eucharist is celebrated, the following prayer may be used afterward.

～ Post-Communion Prayer

People: Most loving God, you are the source of life and our defender in the hour of death. We thank you for feeding us with the spiritual food of the body and blood of Jesus Christ. May we be strengthened to meet the days ahead with hope and newness of life. Grant that we may serve others in your name and to your glory. Bless our sister, _____, and her child; give to them peace in the unity of your love. All this we ask through Jesus Christ. Amen.

～ Benediction

Celebrant: The blessing of God,
the creator of life
be with you this day.

The blessing of God,
the redeemer of abundant love
be with you always.

The blessing of God,
the sanctifier of all,
send you as a blessing to others.

All: So be it.
Alleluia.
Amen.

RITUALS FOR ABORTION

There are three parts to this ritual:

> *Before:* Preparation; the need for courage
> *During:* Friend; the need for support
> *After:* Guilt; the need for forgiveness

~ Before

Friends gather with the woman at her home prior to the abortion. It could be the night, or the morning, before the surgery. They share a simple meal together as a sign of friendship.

After the meal the friends gather in a circle around the woman and lay hands upon her. They may express their feelings and prayers in their own words or say the following together:

We lay our hands upon you in the name of our Savior, Jesus Christ, beseeching God to uphold you and to fill you with grace, that you may know the healing power of God's divine love. We ask God to fill your heart with strength and courage and we give you our love, promising to stand by you through this decision and in the days to come. Amen.

The friends then greet one another with hugs.

~ During

A friend goes with the woman to the place of abortion and stays with her as long as is permitted. Prior to leaving, the friend takes oil, which she has brought with her, and anoints the woman.

On the head, saying: We support your decision.

On the hands, saying: We hold your hands in solidarity and love.

On the womb, saying: We bless you.

The two women hug as a sign of peace between them and all the friends who gathered earlier.

~ After

Friends gather once again with the woman at the time of her choosing. They gather in a circle.

Water is poured from a pitcher into a bowl in front of the woman.

Friend: We wash you with water as a symbol of the tears of mourning, the forgiveness of guilt, and the beginning of a new life for you.

One by one the friends come to the woman, put their hand in the water and place water on her head, her hands, her face, or her feet.

At the end the friends greet one another with hugs, the sign of friendship and peace.

~ ‡ ~

LITANY FOR AIDS SUNDAY

~ ‡ ~

Leader: Gracious God,
You are merciful and loving,
Hear our prayers
on behalf of all who suffer with AIDS:

For all who live in fear of the disease,

People: Grant them peace in their hearts,
Wisdom in the choices they make,
And courage to face the days ahead.

The congregation may offer petitions for persons for whom prayers are desired.

Leader: For all who live with the disease of AIDS,

People: Grant them the gift of your love,
hope for their future,
friends to comfort and sustain them,
the will to live,
and faith that resurrection is a promise for *now*
as well as for eternal life.

The congregation may offer petitions for persons for whom prayers are desired.

Leader: For all who minister to the needs of persons with AIDS,

People: Grant them compassionate hearts,
tenderness and patience in their daily tasks,
and dedication in their ministry to all who suffer.

The congregation may offer petitions for persons for whom prayers are desired.

Leader: For all whose loved ones are affected by AIDS,

People: Grant them hope each day,
an awareness that love is forever binding,
the knowledge that Christ shares their suffering.

The congregation may offer petitions for persons for whom prayers are desired.

Leader: For all who have died of AIDS,

People: Grant them rest eternal;
may light perpetual shine upon them,
may we always remember them in our hearts.

The congregation may offer petitions for persons for whom prayers are desired.

Celebrant: O God of love, whose mercy has always included those whom we have forgotten, those whom we have isolated, and those who suffer: bless we beseech you all who are afflicted with AIDS.

Comfort them in their pain, sustain them by your Holy Spirit in their days of hopelessness that they may engage in living. Receive them into the arms of your mercy in their dying.

Open our hearts to provide for their needs, to take away their isolation, to share their journey of suffering and sorrow as well as hope and joy, and to be present with them in their dying, that no one need suffer or die alone.

Strengthen all who care for those who are ill, that their service may be filled with the tenderness of your compassion and the fullness of your love, that their words and deeds may make your presence a living reality for those whom they serve.

Bless those who mourn the death of their friends and lovers, that they may not be overwhelmed by death but may receive comfort and strength to meet the days ahead with trust and hope in your goodness and mercy; in Jesus' name we pray.

People: Amen.

~ ‡ ~

RITUALS OF DEATH

~ ‡ ~

These rituals may be performed in many ways. Choose the ones most comfortable and appropriate to you and your loved one. There are endless possibilities that will come to your mind as you reflect upon these. The order of the rituals may be varied and repeated according to your needs.

PREPARING FOR DEATH

Expressing love

- Conversations.

- Touching (massage; holding hands; embracing).

- Sharing favorite things (playing music; reading; walks; picking flowers; collecting leaves).

Prayer:

Bless our love, O God the source of love. Help us to share the depth of our love with each other in the last days. Give us the grace to be tender and kind in the midst of stress and the fear of death and loss. Grant that the little things we do together may be signs of the power of love to make us whole and to bond us forever; in the name of Jesus Christ we pray. Amen.

Remembering the blessings of your lives and giving thanks

- Naming what has been of value to the dying person.

- Naming what you'll always remember and value.

- Naming what's been important to each of you.

- Giving thanks for these blessings you have known (talking about them together; writing them down in a letter or booklet; making something together, if possible, e.g., bread, a favorite dish, a scrapbook).

Prayer:

Receive our thanks, O God of love, for this wonderful relationship that we have shared. You have blessed us with commitment, fidelity (friendship), trust, and abiding love. These we have known and expressed in large and small ways. Our lives have been enriched by each of them. Let your continued blessings be upon us, binding us in love when we are no longer together, that those things that we remember in the days to come may continue the joy we have shared; in Jesus Christ's name we pray. Amen.

Sharing special moments

- Things you've always wanted to do but have not done.

- Just being together in stillness, conversation, or activity.

- Enjoying simple things: sunsets, birthdays, etc.

- Naming events to anticipate and live for.

Prayer:

We thank you, O God of love, for the time to engage in special moments that will enrich our memories of love. We thank you for the opportunity to wonder and reflect on the meaning of our love. We thank you for the blessing our relationship has been to our lives. May these moments we have shared be the basis of sharing the love we have known with those in need of such blessing in their lives; in the name of Jesus Christ we pray. Amen.

Doing practical things

- Writing a will.

- Preparing a living will.

- Planning one's funeral (with the family if possible; leave room for others' plans and needs).

- Discussing how and where to die.

Prayer:

Direct us with your grace, O God of love, as we prepare to do the difficult task of planning the practical things we need to do. Strengthen us to say the words so hard to name. Let these objectives draw us deeper in trust and love; in the name of Jesus Christ we pray. Amen.

AT THE TIME OF DEATH

Crying and talking

Too often we hide our tears from one another in order "to protect" the other person. Tears are a sign of love, of how much we shall miss our beloved. Let them flow.

Prayer:

Let our tears of love flow as your love flows over us, O merciful God. Hold us close in your love as we face our parting; in the name of Christ we pray. Amen.

Saying good-bye

Those who are dying often need the permission of the living to die. When it is given it makes it easier to let go of life. The dying is more peaceful and less of a struggle. Sometimes it's possible for a family member to do this and some just can't do it. If the latter is true for you, ask a priest, minister, or someone close to you to help.

Formally:

- Saying prayers or a litany.

- Making Eucharist together.

- Having a priest give the commendation.

> Depart, O Christian soul out of this world;
> In the name of God, who created you;
> In the name of Jesus Christ, who sets you free;
> In the name of the Holy Spirit, who sanctifies you now and
> forever.
> May you rest in peace in the love of God.
> Amen.

Informally:

- "It's okay to go."

- "You can go on your journey."

- "If it's time for you to die, it's all right."

- "You can go now, _____. I'll always love you."

- Whatever words feel most appropriate to you are always the best

Singing: *Singing helps us to relax, for it reminds us of being sung to sleep as a child, or of favorite memories. Music eases pain. To sing someone into their dying, if appropriate to the person and circumstance, is a lovely gift. It helps bond two people when there is nothing the living can "do" and when often the dying can no longer respond.*

Prayer:

As you have blessed us in our loving, bless us in our parting, O God. As nothing can separate us from your love, so let ours be bonded forever; in the name of Christ we pray. Amen.

Washing the body

This is the last direct act of love we have the opportunity to share. It is an intimate act. For some too painful to do, for others it is the perfect act for saying good-bye. Choose what is right for you; trust your feelings and instinct to know what to do.

- Have someone read psalms while the washing is done in silence.

- Use this opportunity to share last words.

- Just touching and being quiet and private is fine.

- The body may be wrapped in a sheet or dressed.

Prayer:

As Jesus' feet were washed in an act of love and in preparation for his burial, so too do we bathe our beloved. Grant to her [him] the joy and peace of salvation; in the name of Jesus Christ we pray. Amen.

When you're not there at the time of death or for the funeral

- Say a prayer or read the burial office at the same hour as the funeral.

- Get out a photo and cry and talk to the one you love.

- Light a candle at a church or at home.

- Share stories with friends.

- Create a ritual of good-bye of your own.

- Read old letters.

- All the above.

Prayer:

Unto God's mercy, protection, and love I commit you, _____. I give thanks for the blessings and love we have shared. May you dwell in peace and in the light of God now and forever. I shall not forget you, I promise; in Christ's name I pray. Amen.

A wake

The need to cry is often stifled by being "in public" at a funeral. A wake is a more intimate and private gathering that permits us to express our grief openly in the company of others who are grieving as well. The sooner we can be in touch with our feelings, the better it is for our grieving process; thus a wake can be helpful.

- Tell stories with friends.

- Share food and drink.

- Look at pictures.

- Comfort one another.

Prayer:

Receive our prayers for _____, O God of love. Grant her [him] rest, peace, and the joy of your presence. Bless _____ and all of us who mourn. Let us not hide from this pain in words or busy actions. Keep us open to the depths of love and our need for one another; in the name of Jesus Christ our Savior we pray. Amen.

Funeral ritual

- Set the context in which you wish all that's said to be heard and understood. This may be done by readings, a family statement, or a homily.

- Name and remember what you will always cherish.

- Express belief in what comes next for your loved one and for you.

- Commit the person you love to God, the earth, and the future.

- Say good-bye (place a flower in the grave; put earth into the grave; stand in silence at the grave and listen to your heart).

Prayer:

Hear our prayers for _____, O God of love. You made us of the dust of the earth, and we have returned her [him] to the earth, to your creation, and committed her to your love. Bless _____ in death as you have been faithful to her in her living. Comfort us who mourn and empower us to commit our short and fragile lives to do your will on earth; in the name of our Savior, Jesus Christ, we pray. Amen.

LATER AND ON ANNIVERSARIES

Remembering and naming aloud

Anniversaries and birthdays are important to mark; they help us to grieve and to begin the process of letting go of the dead and of reconnecting with the living. Letting go doesn't mean forgetting; we never do. The pain and grief are always there in some degree. Making the grief present may be more healing than hiding it.

- Look at old photos.

- Place a special photo in an important place; put flowers beside it.

- Gather friends and share stories.

- Set a place at the table.

- Light a candle.

- Talk to your loved one. (There's nothing "crazy" about doing this. It has helped a lot of people cope with the days ahead.)

- Visit the cemetery.

- Place flowers at the grave.

- Give a gift in memory of your loved one. (This is especially good to do when a special occasion arises like a wedding at which the person is not present and is missed. The gift reminds all of the presence of her love in our hearts and acknowledges our remembrance of her on that occasion.)

- Do something for another in the person's name.

Prayer:

We remember this day _____, and the love with which you blessed us, O God of our creation. Grant that our memories of the wonders and joys of life that we shared may remain clear and as beautiful as they were on the day of their occurrence. May we be forever bonded in your love; in Christ's name we pray. Amen.

Committing to life once again

- Make new relationships; invite others to your home for a meal.

- Discover new involvements; volunteer your time to a worthy cause.

- Learn to live *with* rather than *getting over* grief; talk about the one you love.

- Incorporate the deceased person's values into your own living: undertake a special project that your beloved would have done; choose a value of hers that you can accept as your own.

Prayer:

Hear my prayer, O God of love. Give me the courage to face life again, to make new friendships, commitments, and to risk loving and losing love. Embolden me to reach out to others, to try new things and to do them alone. Let the love that I have known with _____ be my surety that you will always be with me until my life's end. Bless _____ with your eternal love; in the name of Christ I pray. Amen.

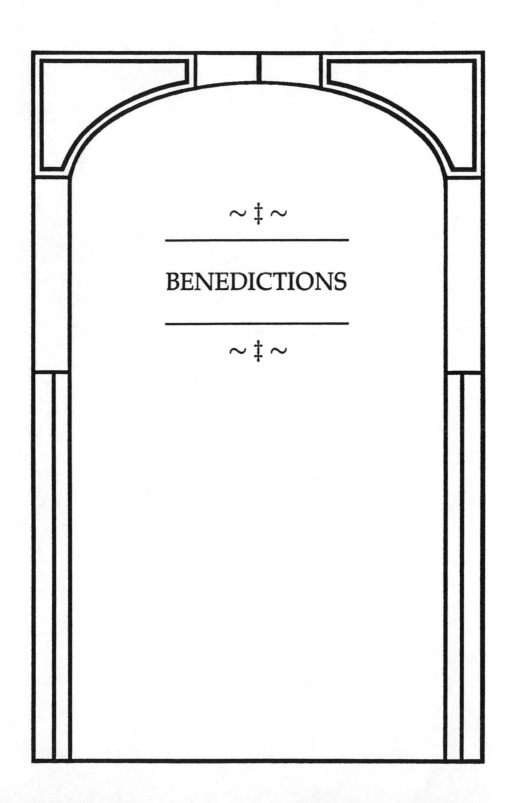

~ ‡ ~

BENEDICTIONS

~ ‡ ~

~ Benediction When the Bishop Is Present

Bishop: The blessing of God,
the Creator of life,
be upon you always.

People: So be it.

Bishop: The blessing of God,
the Redeemer of the world,
be in your words and deeds.

People: So be it.

Bishop: The blessing of God,
the Sanctifier of life,
be with all, now and evermore.

People: So be it. Alleluia! Amen.

~ Benediction for a Special Occasion

Celebrant: The peace of God which passes all understanding keep your hearts and minds in the knowledge and love of God, and of God's Chosen One, Jesus Christ.

The blessing of God who created you,
be with you this *day/night.*

People: Blessed be God.

Celebrant: The blessing of God who redeemed you
be with you always.

People: Blessed be God's holy name.

Celebrant: The blessing of God who sanctifies you
be with you, now and forever.

People: Blessed be God, our Creator, Redeemer, and Sanctifier, throughout all ages. Alleluia! Amen.

∼ An Advent Blessing

The blessing of God,
who has promised
to come into our lives,
be with you today.

The blessing of God,
whose love ransoms us
from all captivity,
be with you forever.

The blessing of God,
whose breath brings new beginnings,
send you forth into the world
to create a new day for the good of all.
Amen.

∼ A Christmas Blessing

The blessing of God,
whose love created
light and darkness,
mystery and wonder,
be with you this day.

The blessing of God,
whose love entered this world
vulnerable, naked, and helpless,
be with you always.

The blessing of God,
whose love burns in your heart,
transforming your living,
send you into the world
to be the incarnation of God's love for others.
Amen.

~ An Epiphany Blessing

The blessing of God,
who created both darkness and light,
be with you today,
that your life may be illumined
by divine Wisdom.

The blessing of God,
who loves you
and restores you to wholeness,
be with you always,
that you may love others
in Christ's name.

The blessing of God,
who sanctifies the breath
of your living,
inspire your words and actions,
thoughts, and feelings,
that you may be the messenger
of God's blessing in this world
today.
Amen.

~ A Lenten Blessing

The blessing of God,
who creates life out of death,
be with you today.

The blessing of God,
who suffers with the sin of this world
and blesses all humankind with grace,
be with you always.

The blessing of God,
who sanctifies
our transformations and turnings,
be with you
as you reveal the power of God's love
to save.
Amen.

～ An Easter Vigil Blessing

The blessing of God,
to whom belongs all power and might,
be with you this night.

The blessing of God,
whose love has the power
to transform our lives
and redeem us from the death of sin,
be with you always.

The blessing of God,
whose Spirit sanctifies life,
send you into the world
to create hope for all.
Amen.

～ An Easter Blessing

The blessing of God,
who creates life,
be upon you
as you celebrate life.

The blessing of God,
who restores life,
be upon you
as you seek new life.

The blessing of God,
who sanctifies life,
be upon you
as you give life to others.
Amen.

~ A Pentecost Blessing

The blessing of God,
whose love creates new life
and whose fire burns away our impurities,
be with you in your journey of life.

The blessing of God,
whose love has the power
to transform our living
from old habits into new hope,
be with you always.

The blessing of God,
whose Spirit blesses our spirit
with wisdom and vision,
embolden you to proclaim
the Good News of God's love to all.
Amen.

~ A Blessing at a Funeral

Celebrant: The blessing of God,
whose love created all things
and gave us life,
be with you this day.

People: Thanks be to God.

Celebrant: The blessing of God,
whose love is victorious over death,
be with you always.

People: Thanks be to God for ever and ever.

Celebrant: The blessing of God,
whose love restores us to life,
enable you to comfort one another.

People: Thanks be to God. Alleluia! Amen.

～ A Blessing

The peace of God,
which passes all understanding,
keep your hearts and minds
in the knowledge and love of God
and of God's Chosen One, Jesus Christ.

The blessing of God,
whose breath gave life to the world,
be in all you speak this day.

The blessing of God,
whose love reconciles all who are divided,
be with you as you seek to heal
the brokenness around you.

The blessing of God,
whose Spirit sanctifies life,
be with you as you go forth into the world
to bless others with God's love.

So be it! Amen.

～ A Blessing

Celebrant: The blessing of God,
who gave birth
to all that has life,
be upon you
this *day/night.*

People: Blessed be God.

Celebrant: The blessing of God,
who loved the world so much
as to die for it,
be upon you
as you seek to love others.

People: Blessed be God's holy name.

Celebrant: The blessing of God
who inspires all life
be upon you
as you live out your days.

People: Blessed be God
now and forever. Amen.

～ A Blessing

Celebrant: The blessing of God whose love embraces all be with you this day and forever.

People: Thanks be to God.

Celebrant: The blessing of God whose grace forgives our sin be with you this day and forever.

People: Thanks be to God. So be it.

Celebrant: The blessing of God whose Spirit inspires our living be with you this day and forever.

People: Thanks be to God. Alleluia! Amen.

～ A Blessing

Celebrant: Blessed are you, Mother of all life.

People: Blessed be your name, forever and ever.

Celebrant: Blessed are you, Father and Creator.

People: Blessed be your name, forever and ever.

Celebrant: Blessed are you, Redeemer of the world.

People: Blessed be your name, forever and ever.

Celebrant: Blessed are you, Sanctifier of life.

People: Blessed be your name, forever and ever.

Celebrant: The blessing of God, Source of our salvation, be with you always.

People: Blessed be God's holy name, forever and ever.

~ Benediction for a Marriage

The blessing of God,
who created you male and female,
be with you as you become one flesh.

The blessing of God,
whose love transforms all things,
be with you as you fulfill your vows.

The blessing of God,
whose Spirit inspires all love,
be with you now and forever. Amen.

~ Benediction for an Anniversary

The blessing of God,
whose love gave you life,
be with you this day.

The blessing of God,
whose love makes all things new,
be with you on this special occasion.

The blessing of God,
whose love gives us hope for tomorrow,
be with you now and always. Amen.

~ Benediction for a Special Occasion

Celebrant: The blessing of God,
whose love created all life,
be with you this day.

People: Praise and thanks to God who loves us.

Celebrant: The blessing of God,
whose love redeems our life,
be with you in all things.

People: Praise and thanks to God who loves us.

Celebrant: The blessing of God,
whose love inspires our being,
be with you now and always.

People: Praise and thanks to God who loves us.
For ever and ever. Amen.

~ Blessing for a Couple
Who Are Getting a Divorce

The blessing of God whose breath gives life
be with you always.
The blessing of God whose
love is forgiving
set you free from guilt and despair.
The blessing of God
who sanctifies your living
be with you this day,
to lead you to a new life
of hope, peace, love, and service.
May God be praised and glorified through your lives,
now and forever. Amen.

~ Benediction for Martin Luther King Sunday

God, who created the diversity of humankind
including black, white, red, and yellow,
bless you today.

God, who has reconciled us to one another
and whose love is the source of our healing,
bless you always.

God, who transforms us from death to life
and who gives us a new heart,
send you into the city to bring hope
and to build koinonia. Amen.

~ Benediction for an Ordination

Bishop: The blessing of God,
who created both darkness and light,
be with you today,

People: That our lives may be illumined
by divine Wisdom.

Bishop: The blessing of God,
who loves you
and who restores you to wholeness
be with you always,

People: That we may love others
in Christ's name.

Bishop: The blessing of God,
who sanctifies the breath of your living
inspire your words and actions,
thoughts, and feelings,

People: That we may be the messengers
of God's blessing in this world
today and every day. Amen.

~ A Stewardship Blessing

God, who created the vineyard in which we dwell,
bless you this day with faithfulness.

God, who has set us free from sin and death,
open your hearts to repentance and the gift of salvation.

God, whose Spirit empowers us with grace,
send you into the world as stewards of God's love
that all may share in the abundance which has been given.
Amen.

~ A General Blessing

God has breathed the breath of life within you.
Blessed be God, and God's blessing be upon you.

God has saved us from sin and death through grace.
Blessed be God, and God's blessing be upon you.

God has empowered us to serve in God's name.
Blessed be God, and God's blessing be upon you.